American Lit Relit

American Lit Relit

A short history of American literature for long-suffering students, for teachers who manage to keep one chapter ahead of the class, and for all those who, no longer being in school, can happily sink back into illiteracy

by
Richard Armour

With illustrious illustrations by
Campbell Grant

McGraw-Hill Book Company · New York · Toronto · London

AUTHOR'S NOTE

There are no half-truths in this book,
but the reader may occasionally come upon
a truth-and-a-half.

R.A.

I

The Beginnings of American Literature

WHEN did American literature begin? Where did it begin? Who began it? These are among the many questions that literary historians have raised, and lowered, over the years. Such questions cannot be taken lightly, nor can they be answered "Well, yes and no."

The first writers in America were probably Indians, writing for "little" magazines made of pieces of birch bark and being paid so much wampum per word. If one could leaf through one of these early journals, one might pick up some interesting ideas.[1] But all, alas, are gone, traded to white settlers as firewood in exchange for firewater. Other early writings, in the form of smoke signals, have fared no better. Efforts to deposit them in libraries led to poor visibility, fits of coughing, and mass resignations by cataloguers.

So we must turn to those who, although writing in America, were born in England and could not even become naturalized until after the American Revolution, which was more than a hundred and fifty years off. Though now considered American authors, they thought themselves

---

[1] As well as an occasional splinter.

Early writing

English and expected to be included in anthologies somewhere between Shakespeare and Milton. Had they realized that they were, instead, beginning American literature and going to be read by thousands of high school and college students, they might have been more careful about their spelling.

Captain John Smith

Captain John Smith is sometimes called the father of American literature. A professional soldier in his youth, he became a writer when "he exchanged his sword for a pen." Whether he had been trying unsuccessfully to dip his sword into an inkwell we do not know, but he was obviously a poor trader.

Smith went to America in 1607 with the Virginia Company, being a stockholder and not having much confidence in the management.[1] While others were busy founding Jamestown, he wrote a book with the catchy title of *A True Relation of Such Occurrences and Accidents of Note as Hath Hapned in Virginia*. As he anticipated, many bought the book to read about the accidents and find out who got hurt. Others were simply curious as to the meaning of *Hapned*.

Captain John Smith's greatest contribution to American literature was his story, in *The Generall Historie of Virginia*, of how he was captured by the Indian leader, King Powhatan, and saved from having his brains beaten out when Pocahontas, the King's favorite daughter, "got his head in her armes, and laid her owne upon his to save him from death." It was a touching scene, her head touching his, and many doubt it ever happened. Captain John Smith

[1] Going into stocks, in those days, meant putting the hands and feet through holes in a thick piece of wood.

Touching scene

may not have invented the short story, but he made an important contribution to the tall tale.

William Byrd

Before we leave the early writers of the South, mention should be made of Colonel William Byrd, also of Virginia, who was a lesser writer but outranked Captain John Smith militarily. William Byrd was the son of a wealthy Virginia

William Byrd

landowner to whom workers and neighbors were always bringing presents labeled "For the Byrds." He was educated in England, where, we are told, "he was called to the bar," apparently by some roistering friends. Eventually he staggered back to Virginia, inherited his father's estates, and became so rich that he had no reason to write, and yet did.

Most of Byrd's writings were in the form of diaries, which caused him to be referred to as "the American Pepys." [1] His use of capitals is somewhat perplexing, as when he writes, "We all kept Snug in our several apartments till Nine, except Miss Thecky, who was the Housewife of the Family." The reader at first thinks Snug is a dog or a cat, a favorite of everyone. This same Miss Thecky turns up in Byrd's description of a walk he took on Governor Spotswood's estate: "Just behind was a cover'd Bench, where Miss Thecky often sat and bewail'd her Virginity." Interestingly, she lamented not the loss of it but still having it. This, it must be remembered, was the South, not New England.

Byrd's most important work was his *History of the Dividing Line,* a survey of a survey. He was a member of the commission that determined where Virginia stopped and North Carolina began. The one jog in an otherwise straight border, just above Winston, North Carolina, was caused when Byrd was scribbling in his notebook when he should have been peering through his transit. [2]

[1] So far as is known, Pepys has never been called "the English Byrd."
[2] "Sick transit," said Byrd later, trying to shift the blame from himself.

II

Early New England Writers

ONE of the passengers on the *Mayflower* was William Bradford, who wrote from morning till night all the way over, hoping to keep his mind off the motion of the ship. Once ashore, he began writing, in what he called "a plaine stile" (he was a perceptive self-critic), a history entitled *Of Plimouth Plantation*. The following is an example of his plaine stile and fancy spellinge: "Some became souldiers, others tooke upon them farr viages." I think a farr viage is the same as a longg trippe, but don't use me as an authority.

Even more remarkable than Bradford's literary achievements was the fact that he was elected governor of Plymouth thirty-one times. If governors had served a four-year term, Bradford, who was elected at the age of thirty-one, would have held office until he was 155.[1]

Not to be outdone by the Governor of Plymouth, Governor Winthrop of Massachusetts Bay wrote a *Journal* which is full of accounts of fires, pestilences, drownings, witchcraft, Indian massacres, and sundry evils and afflictions dear to the heart of a Puritan. Describing the murder of a nice old planter by a band of Indians, Winthrop wrote: "They found John Oldham stark naked, his head cleft to

---

[1] They did *not* serve a four-year term.

the brains, and his hands and legs cut as if they had been cutting them off, and yet warm." Had the rescuers arrived a few minutes earlier, they would have witnessed a lively scene, forsooth.

One writer who was not a Puritan was Thomas Morton, a cutup who lived in a settlement appropriately named Merry Mount. He gave gunpowder and liquor (a bad combination) to the Indians, whom he thought more Chris-

A merry Puritan

15

tian than the Christians, and in the spring of 1627 erected a Maypole, just for the heck of it. The revelry of Morton and his friends around the Maypole, tossing flowers into the air and performing other pagan rites, was shocking to behold. To annoy the Puritans still further, he wrote *The New English Canaan,* a wicked book full of four-letter words (such as *hill* and *deem*), and for his misdeeds was exiled to Maine.

Almost as harshly treated was Roger Williams, who was forced to flee to Rhode Island after writing *The Bloody Tenent,* about an unfortunate fellow who fell behind in rent payments to his Puritan landlord. Williams, who had such radical ideas as a belief in tolerance, independent thinking, and kindness to Indians, was born too soon.[1]

Bay Psalm Book

Poetry began with the *Bay Psalm Book,* which has the distinction of being the first book published in America, publishers being more willing to take a chance on a book of poems in those days. Only a few copies have survived, and it is possible, by examining the word order of such lines as

> The Lord to mee a shepheard is,
> Want therefore shall not I,

to guess why. It was written not by a single author but by a committee, which explains everything.

[1] In fact, he would have been born too soon if he were living today.

Anne Bradstreet

Though not a governor herself, Anne Bradstreet was both the daughter of a governor and the wife of a governor of Massachusetts. She therefore passed the test for being a Colonial writer with flying colors. While caring for her eight children, she somehow found time to write hundreds of poems, many of them collected in a volume called *The Tenth Muse, Lately Sprung up in America.* The rest of the title, containing such phrases as *Severall Poems, compiled with great variety of Wit and Learning, full of delight, etc.,* was, in later editions, transferred to the jacket as a blurb.

Aware of the fact that women were supposed to do the housework and leave poetry and such manly activities to men, she wrote:

> I am obnoxious to each carping tongue
> Who says my hand a needle better fits.

But, having pricked her finger with a needle once too often, she decided she was not cut out for that sort of thing and turned to poetry.

One of Mrs. Bradstreet's poems contains these lines descriptive of her husband:

> My head, my heart, mine Eyes, my life, nay more,
> My joy, my Magazine of earthly store.

Her husband, overwhelmed, expired shortly thereafter.

Michael Wigglesworth

A name to be reckoned with, and not easily forgotten, is Michael Wigglesworth, whose most popular work was a long poem entitled *The Day of Doom*.[1] Wigglesworth's purpose was to terrify sinners, and he succeeded admirably. Nonetheless, they were so eager to see what lay ahead that

Day of Doom

they could hardly put the book down, except when they shook so hard they dropped it. Probably the most memorable part of the poem describes the damnation of infants who died before they had time to become regular church-goers. These tiny tots "from the womb unto the tomb were straightway carried," according to Wigglesworth, who could not help admiring an efficient funeral arrangement. As a concession to their immaturity and being away from home for the first time, they were given "the easiest room in Hell." While people read his poem, Wigglesworth, also a physician, thoughtfully stood by with a hypo and a sedative.

[1] The alliteration is worth note in passing (the course).

III

Later Early New England Writers

COLONIAL literature was greatly influenced, though not necessarily for the better, by the Mathers. Their names were Increase and Cotton, not to be confused with Decrease and Dacron.

Increase Mather

Increase Mather, a man of average size, was always drawing himself up to his full height so impressively that he seemed to be getting larger while you watched, which may explain his first name. He was a Godly Sort. Things didn't happen by chance, he thought, but were caused by Somebody Up There, as he made abundantly clear in *An Essay for the Recording of Illustrious Providences*. Interestingly, all of these Providences were in Massachusetts, no mention being made of the one in Rhode Island.

In this book he tells with a straight face (and when Increase had a straight face it was really straight) about a family that "was strangely disquieted by a Demon." "In the morning," he writes, "there were five great Stones and Bricks by an *invisible hand* thrown in the west end of the house while the Mans Wife was making the Bed, the Bedstead was lifted up from the floor, and the Bedstaff flung out of the Window, and a Cat was hurled at him; a long staff danced up and down in the Chimney; a burnt Brick and a piece of weatherboard were thrown in at the Window," and so on. This continued for weeks, and why the family didn't do something about it, such as call the police or move to a more congenial neighborhood, is the greatest mystery of all.

Increase Mather believed himself one of the elect, and in view of his political successes may have been right.[1] An M.A. from Trinity College, Dublin, and for sixteen years president of Harvard, he not only believed in demons but also took part enthusiastically in the Salem witch trials, thus proving that education need not be a handicap.

Cotton Mather

Cotton Mather, Increase's son, entered Harvard at the age of eleven and was too light for the football team. He

[1] He was not only right but far right, one of the most conservative conservatives of his day.

Entered Harvard at eleven

wrote some 470 books and pamphlets, full of the Devil and italics. Indeed, he wrote so much that we are inclined to believe his biographer when he says, "There are two Cotton Mathers—one the actual man and the other the figure of legend." There may even have been half a dozen, considering all those words.

Like his father, he was a great believer in witches, spooks, and the like, of which he wrote in *Wonders of the Invisible World*. Witches, he was certain, were engaged in the "Hellish Design of *Bewitching* and *Ruining* our Land." Unlike witch hunters of today, he failed to mention the State Department or the Supreme Court.

Nevertheless, when Cotton failed to succeed his father as president of Harvard, it grieved him sorely. In a fit of pique, he founded Yale.

The New England Primer

Rising to even greater heights than the poetry of Anne Bradstreet or the *Bay Psalm Book* was *The New England Primer*. This contained not only the famous couplet,

> In Adam's fall
> We sinnèd all,

but the even more beautiful triplet,

> Young Obadias,
> David, Josias,
> All were pious.

All New England books were prim, but this one was primmer.

Samuel Sewall

A valuable picture of Colonial life is to be found in Samuel Sewall's *Diary*. But for this, we would not know that on July 6, 1685, "An Indian was branded in court and had a piece of his ear cut off for burglary." How large a piece probably depended on the size of the theft. This, by the way, compares favorably with the treatment of Indians for the next couple of centuries, when their land was taken from them although they were allowed to keep their ears.

One of Sewall's most interesting entries, that of October 6, 1688, has to do with another Indian, who, apparently on a whim, or a dare, hanged himself in the Brewhouse, whereupon "The Coroner sat upon him, having a jury, and ordered his burial by the highway with a stake through his grave." This graphic picture of the coroner and the jury sitting on the dead Indian until he could be buried is as memorable as anything in Colonial literature.

Jonathan Edwards

To close this chapter on a happier note, we make brief mention of Jonathan Edwards, a preacher in Northampton, Massachusetts, whose greatest sermon was "Sinners in the Hands of an Angry God." It was sure-fire, as well as hell-fire, depicting an eternity of damnation so vividly that after a few minutes he had his parishioners emptying their pockets into the collection plate and writhing on the floor. At heart a kindly man, Edwards withstood the urge to horsewhip them while they were in this helpless position. He was the founder of a religious movement known as The Great Awakening, no one in his congregation being able to stay asleep long while he was painting such a colorful picture of the Hereafter.

For twenty-one years Jonathan Edwards continued his preaching in Northampton. When he was not preaching, he was writing or wandering in the woods, where he enjoyed watching spiders spin their webs. Had Smith College

Spider watcher

been founded somewhat earlier, one wonders what a Jonathan Edwards sermon on Changing Campus Mores or Sex and the Single Girl would have sounded like.

IV

Benjamin Franklin

A GREAT change in American literature came with Benjamin Franklin. Unlike Jonathan Edwards, who believed in saving souls, the more practical Franklin believed in saving money. "A penny saved is a penny earned," he said—this being before the income tax, Blue Cross, and Social Security, when 100 per cent of one's pay was take-home pay. At any rate Franklin gave an earthy touch to American letters.

Ben was the son of a candle-maker in Boston, and from him he learned how foolish and wasteful it is to burn your candle at both ends. He wanted to run off to sea, but his father bound him to his brother, a printer, to prevent him from doing so. All of this, and much more, he tells in his

Printer's devil

Benjamin Franklin

Autobiography, the most memorable part of which is his account of how he ran away from Boston and walked down the main street of Philadelphia with three rolls, one under each arm and eating the other. All his busy life, he had his hands full. The starchy diet also explains his pudgy figure.

The *Autobiography,* which today would be entitled *How to Become Rich and Famous through Hard Work,* was the first rags-to-riches success story in American literature, preaching industry and thrift and totally disregarding the American dream, which is to get rich quick by marrying the boss's daughter, making a killing in stocks, or holding the winning ticket in a lottery. Franklin also tells of his efforts to achieve "moral perfection," which is no piddling goal. He even includes a list of the thirteen virtues and a chart he used to score himself daily. Anyone who wishes can make up a similar chart and see how he is doing on such things as Temperance, Frugality, Industry, Sincerity, Chastity, and Humility. The chart can be carried in one's wallet, along with one's driver's license and credit cards, and whipped out for the addition of a black mark at each infraction. It might be advisable to make the columns somewhat wider than Franklin did, allowing more space for black marks.

25

Besides being a writer and a printer,[1] the versatile Franklin was, among other things, a statesman and an inventor. He was, for example, the inventor of bifocals, and no wonder, for it is said that he "wrote always with his eye on his audience," and the eyestrain forced him to desperate measures. Many of his essays on scientific subjects, such as electricity, kite-making, and the cause and cure of smoky chimneys, were written in the form of letters to his friends, who would rather have him write about what he was doing than come over and demonstrate, messing up the sink and blowing all the fuses.

One of Franklin's most popular works is *Poor Richard's Almanac*, in which he pronounces such memorable pronouncements as "Never leave that till tomorrow which you can do today," "Be ashamed to be idle," and "He that riseth late, must trot all day." All of these precepts are easy to agree with, so long as agreement is all that is expected.

But Franklin, the moralist, also had a sharp eye for the ladies. Take this passage from *Reflections on Courtship and Marriage:* "Let us survey the morning dress of some women. Downstairs they come, pulling up their ungartered, dirty stockings; slipshod, with naked heels peeping out; no stays or other conveniency, but all flip-flop . . . unwashed, teeth furred, and eyes crusted." These, of course, are married women. Unmarried women are another matter, and an essay that would never have been written by Cotton Mather or Jonathan Edwards is Franklin's "Advice to a Young Man on the Choice of a Mistress." Ben spent a good deal of time in Paris as Minister

---

[1] A good combination if you want to be published.

to France, and had been around. This essay is to be found in a volume entitled *The All-Embracing Doctor Franklin*.

"Men and melons are hard to know," Franklin says in his *Almanac,* and women are also hard to figure out. But Franklin didn't suggest thumping them to see whether they were ripe. He preferred squeezing.

V

Writers of
the Revolutionary Period

THOUGH some were favorable to the British, most writers, according to one authority, "were behind the colonists in their struggle for freedom." How far behind, this literary historian does not say, but probably, during such bloody battles as Lexington, Bunker Hill, and Brandywine, several miles at least and holed up in a bulletproof library.

Thomas Paine

One of those who stirred up the patriotism of the colonists was Thomas Paine, an English corset-maker who emigrated to America after going bankrupt. What went wrong with corset-making we do not know. Mayhap a shortage of whalebone.

Paine championed independence of the colonies in a pamphlet entitled *Common Sense.* Answering those who maintained that, since the colonies had prospered under England, they should continue this connection, he sneered, "We may as well assert that because a child has thrived upon milk, it is never to have meat." This was a persuasive

Decided to emigrate

argument, convincing everyone except a few vegetarians. As for the fears of some that war against England would be costly and might even mean going in debt, Paine cried fervently, "No nation ought to be without a debt!" [1] The cautious souls were properly ashamed of themselves and resolved never again to be stingy with the government's money.

But Paine's most important contribution to morale was *The Crisis*, which he brought out in installments to keep up the suspense and because he was commenting on the progress of the war and could not get ahead of the fighting. Soldiers who otherwise would have gone AWOL stayed in camp rather than miss the next part, which might contain some such sentence as "These are the times that try men's souls," which was obviously headed straight for Bartlett's *Familiar Quotations*. Or they stood up in full sight of the enemy, engrossed in such turns of phrase as "The harder the conflict, the more glorious the triumph"

[1] Tom Paine, thou should'st be living at this hour.

and "What we obtain too cheap, we esteem too lightly."
There was no doubt about it, the man could write.

Washington ordered *The Crisis* read to his troops at
Valley Forge, particularly the bit about the "summer soldier and the sunshine patriot," which gave his men, tromp-
ing around in the snow and blowing on their fingers, a nice
warm feeling.

Revolutionary Songs and Ballads

Most of the popular songs of the Revolution were
anonymous, no one with any sense of rhyme, meter, punctuation, or pride being willing to admit authorship. Take
for example these lines from "The Pennsylvania Song":

> What! can those British tyrants think,
>   Our fathers cross'd the main,
> And savage foes and dangers met,
>   To be enslav'd by them?

This, as the reader must have noticed, causes one to wonder
whether *main* should be pronounced "mem" or *them* be
pronounced "thain." One anthologist, while including such
songs as American literature, says, "At first blush they may
not seem like poetry." After the second or third blush,
supposedly, they improve, or the reader becomes less
critical. Readers who turn pale should go out for a breath
of fresh air.

The songs and ballads of the Revolution threw a scare
into the British, causing them to show the whites of their
eyes at Bunker Hill.

Philip Freneau

One poet of this period who was willing to attach his name to his poems was Philip Freneau, who wrote of simple things like William Wordsworth. "With Freneau," says one critic while Anne Bradstreet turns over in her grave, "American poetry begins." Speaking of graves, one of Freneau's best-known poems is "The Indian Burying Ground," in which he describes the Indian custom of burying their dead sitting up instead of lying down. Not only did the Indian sit up in his grave, but with

> His bow, for action ready bent,
> And arrow, with a head of stone,

he was on the alert, ready for anything. One must pity the unsuspecting archeologist who breaks in upon such a scene, the sitting Indian drawing a bead on him.

In addition to his serious poetry, Freneau wrote some devastating satires against the British. One of them, "A Prophecy," begins:

> When a certain great king, whose initial is G.,
> Shall force stamps upon paper, and folks to drink tea. . . .

Most readers got the idea, even guessing who *G.* was, though they were forced to admire Freneau's subtlety.

The Hartford Wits

The Hartford Wits, also called the Connecticut Pranksters, were a group of Yale men, notably Timothy Dwight,

31

T. Dwight: a Connecticut prankster

John Trumbull, and Joel Barlow. Dwight, in fact, became president of Yale, though Barlow defected and wrote *The Columbiad*, a tribute to another ivy-covered institution.

One of Dwight's works, *The Triumph of Infidelity*, was a great disappointment to admirers of *Lady Chatterley's Lover*, since it turned out to be a defense of Calvinistic theology. Trumbull passed the entrance requirements for Yale at the age of seven, but was not admitted until he was thirteen and able to see over his desk. He is famous for a long humorous poem, *M'Fingal*, about a Tory who made lengthy speeches against the Revolution and was tarred and feathered in the end, or, to quote from the poem,

> Glued by the tar to his rear applied,
> Like barnacle on vessel's side.

Such uproarious lines as these are supposed to have "sent men into Washington's army laughing," though George soon wiped that smile off their faces.

As for Barlow, he won his reputation as a wit with his poem, *The Hasty-Pudding*, describing a dessert which can be prepared in half the time it takes to read Barlow's epic. At the end of the poem, Barlow is so sure he has the reader drooling that he says, "Fear not to slaver, 'tis no deadly sin," and hands him a napkin. However the reader needs nothing of the sort, having fallen to sleep before the end of the first canto. Barlow's wittiest writings, it might be added, were published after his death, or posthumorously.

George Washington

George Washington set many precedents, which, as the first President, he was in a good position to do.[1] One was established when he became a writer. Ever since, many

A literary President

Presidents have become writers, while very few writers have become Presidents.[2] The fact that Washington was President of the United States probably helped him find a

[1] He might well be referred to as Precedent Washington.
[2] As one said, on being urged to run, "I would rather write than be President."

33

publisher for speeches, letters, and messages to Congress, none of which had much of a plot line.

Critics have commented on the forcefulness of Washington's prose style, one scholar going so far as to say that his writings "show no loss of vigor as he neared his end." Washington still had the energy, at the close of a ten-page letter, to sign his name with a flourish. As for the beginning of his letters, he often comes forth with a flash of brilliance such as, in an epistle of May 22, 1782: "I have read with attention the sentiments you have submitted to my perusal." This is unquestionably more literary than "Yours of the 19th inst. received."

Of course the most famous of Washington's writings is his Farewell Address, which was written by Alexander Hamilton. That Washington could not have been the author is indicated by the next-to-last paragraph, in which he states: "Though, in reviewing the incidents of my administration, I am unconscious [1] of intentional error, I am nevertheless too sensible of my defects not to think it probable that I may have committed many errors." For a President to say that he might have made a mistake is unthinkable. But the speech, we are told, bears "the stamp of Washington's character." Thus it should be of interest both to students of literature and to philatelists.

Some sticklers believe that the Farewell Address, written on Washington's leaving the Presidency and moving to Mount Vernon, should have been called his Forwarding Address.

---

[1] There is a temptation to pause here, but the reader should hurry on through the sentence.

St. John de Crèvecoeur

A Frenchman who came to America before the Revolution, Crèvecoeur [1] bought a farm in Orange County, N.Y. and wrote a book entitled *Letters from an American Farmer*, in which he told all about the birds and the bees, without pulling his punches. He made farming sound so idyllic that many left the city and bought a few hundred acres of rocky land, where they interrupted their manure-shoveling only to write threatening letters to Crèvecoeur. After getting into trouble with both the Revolutionists and the British, the former thinking him a Tory and the latter thinking him a spy, he returned to France, where he got along fine.

In one of the chapters of *Letters from an American Farmer* he asks the question, "What is an American?" It is a good question, which Crèvecoeur answers in about six thousand words. Apparently it didn't occur to him to say, "An American is a person who lives in America." We can be thankful that Crèvecoeur did not undertake writing a dictionary.

Back in Paris, the author of *Lettres d'un Cultivateur Américain* became a celebrity, relating his adventures in the wilderness to Frenchmen who dreamed of going to America and becoming noble savages. He was willing to hold forth on the idyllic life of farm and forest, in any café or salon, as long as he had a comfortable chair and his wineglass was kept filled.

[1] Crèvecoeur, despite his years in America, never lost his accent. It will be found, even today, over the first *e*.

VI

The Early Novel

THE first full-length novel written in America by an American was *The Power of Sympathy*, which was published anonymously in 1789. Other events in the same year, such as the fall of the Bastille, tended to crowd it off the front pages. However, being about illicit love affairs, a narrow escape from incest, and suicide, it got the American novel off to a good start.

The tradition was carried on by Charles Brockden Brown, who has the distinction of being the first American to make his living with his pen. Up to this time Americans relied upon the shovel and the axe, neither of which is very handy for writing.[1]

Brown was a brooding, introspective fellow, who liked to take solitary walks late at night in the hope of getting material for his books. He might be lucky enough to meet a ghost, or at least a thug. Today he is remembered chiefly for *Wieland*, a novel in which Wieland is driven insane and urged by a ventriloquist to murder his wife and children and does.[2] On behalf of the ventriloquist, a chap named Carwin, it must be said that he also persuades Wieland, who has escaped from a lunatic asylum, not to kill

---

[1] See the muckrakers.

[2] That last word is a verb. He did not kill any female deer.

his sister but to do something humane, for once, and stab himself.

Those who find *Wieland* too spooky for their taste may prefer such novels as *Arthur Mervyn* and *Ormond,* both of which are set in Philadelphia at the time of an epidemic of yellow fever. The heroes and heroines of both books are so virtuous that the reader may think them a little unreal. But the pestilence is so realistic that, as one critic has said, "it seems to rise from the very page." Readers who fear contagion should wear face masks.

Charles Brockden Brown died in 1810, "pointing the way to Hawthorne and Poe." Not only was this an unusual position in which to die, but neither of these writers was ready to take directions, Poe being a baby and Hawthorne a child of six. The whole thing was pretty eerie, and members of the family shook their heads as they gently lowered Brown's hand to his side and buried him.[1]

---

[1] Though in his novels Brown was carried away by yellow fever, in real life, or death, he was carried off by tuberculosis and six pallbearers.

VII

Early Drama

SOME of the earliest American plays were tragedies, as even the authors were forced to admit when they closed down after a short run. The first comedy, however, was *The Contrast*, written in 1787 by Royall Tyler. One amusing incident in it is when Jonathan, a hayseed servant, goes to a play without knowing it is a play, and when the curtain goes up thinks he is looking into the house next door. Since this was long before the invention of the picture window, it was a rare treat for Peeping Jon.

The contrast in *The Contrast* is between a two-fisted, patriotic American and a one-fisted, unpatriotic Anglo-

The Contrast

phile. Tyler subtly hints the difference between the two characters when he names one of them Manly and the other Dimple. What makes the play a comedy is that the heroine, Maria, who in Act I is engaged to Dimple, in Act V is won by Manly. There is something funny about all this?

When *The Contrast* was played in Boston in 1792, it was advertised as "A Moral Lecture in Five Parts." Bostonians who sneaked in, knowing it was really a play, were careful not to laugh.

William Dunlap

The country's first professional dramatist was William Dunlap, and his discovery that a living could be made out of writing plays had a profound influence on the course of American drama. More people took up writing drama as a way of making a living and starved to death.[1]

It is worthy of note that Dunlap, the first professional dramatist, was a close friend of Charles Brockden Brown, the first professional novelist. When they entered a building together there was always a bit of bowing and scraping while each insisted to the other, "You first!" Each encouraged the other in his writing, Brown hoping Dunlap would stick to the drama and Dunlap hoping Brown would stick to the novel. Times were hard enough without competition.

Dunlap's first play was *The Father,* later revised and retitled *The Father of an Only Child* when it looked as if the title character, a loudmouth named Mr. Racket, would

[1] What many of these dramatists did not know was that Dunlap managed the leading company of actors and owned the theater in which his plays were produced.

have no more children. *The Italian Father* is a later play of Dunlap's and not, as might be supposed, an Italian translation of the same play. In all, Dunlap wrote twenty-nine plays, not all of them about fathers. Many have not survived, but then neither has Dunlap, who died in 1839.

John Howard Payne

It may come as a surprise to some that John Howard Payne, the author of the popular song "Home, Sweet Home," was a playwright. If so, it will come as even more of a surprise that Payne was also an actor, American consul to Tunis, and for a while an occupant of debtor's prison in London.[1] In addition, he is said to have haunted the Federal Theater, in Boston.

Payne's most successful play was *Brutus*, a tragedy produced in 1819. Americans, who had not beheld blood flowing in the streets since the War of 1812, flocked to see it. They loved the scene in which Queen Tullia rides her chariot over the dead body of her father, whom she had murdered, and

The gore was dashed
From the hot wheels up to her diadem.

The play made quite a splash.

[1] See remarks, above, on writing plays as a way of making a living.

40

VIII

Widening Horizons

W E now come to a period of widening horizons. Every morning people would rush outdoors to look. "A little wider today, don't you think?" they would ask each other hopefully. What was responsible for this fascinating

Widening horizons

development is a matter for scientific rather than literary inquiry, but everyone agreed that it was a Good Thing.

Whether or not this horizon-widening caused writers to write better, it is quite evident from examining the complete works of Washington Irving and James Fenimore Cooper that it caused them to write more. Perhaps the additional light coming into their studies enabled them to stay at their desks for longer periods.

Washington Irving

One of the outstanding writers of this new era, which began early in the nineteenth century, was Washington Irving. He was destined to give a new setting to American letters because he was born in New York City instead of Boston or Philadelphia like most of his predecessors. Irving got his first name from George Washington, of whom he wrote a five-volume biography to express his gratitude.

Irving often wrote about the past, being interested in legends and history. In his *Knickerbocker's History of New York* he wrote of the days when New York was not New York but New Amsterdam and when "every woman stayed at home, read the Bible, and wore pockets." Those were happy times. Irving's *History* was, as the author said, a book to be "thumbed and chuckled over by the family fireside" and, in the years since it was published in 1809, many a side has become sore from laughing and many a thumb from thumbing. The book was so popular that a group of imitators established the Knickerbocker School, writing in short pants.[1]

Another of his works, *The Sketch Book,* surprised many purchasers, who opened it expecting to find drawings and were sadly disappointed. They did, however, find some of the first American short stories. One of these is "Rip Van Winkle," about a man who went to sleep for twenty years, which is the equivalent of getting his eight hours 21,900 times. He awoke feeling rested.

Still another story in *The Sketch Book* is "The Legend of Sleepy Hollow," about a headless Horseman who scared

[1] Also known as the Breathless School.

the wits out of Ichabod Crane and many a reader. The Horseman was said to be the ghost of a Hessian trooper "whose head had been carried away by a cannon ball." It is a spooky story, and some people feel that it was Irving who got carried away and lost his head.

Irving spent many years abroad, part of the time as Minister to Spain, and came home with books, paintings, tapestries, ashtrays, and an international point of view. This is the more remarkable when we recall that "the Atlantic was immensely broader in those days than now." Irving was fifty-nine days making his first crossing, and thought he would *never* get there.

Thought he would never get there

In 1842, we are told, when he was in England on his way to Spain, "Queen Victoria had already been five years on the throne." Irving, who wrote a number of essays about British customs, probably thought it worth a stopover to see this indomitable sovereign, before she yielded to the entreaties of her worried subjects that she get down and walk around a little to keep up the circulation.[1]

[1] Of course she may have stood up now and then. In that long, full skirt, no one could be sure.

Irving's versatility as a writer enabled him to "summon up either laughter or tears." An example of his ability to give the tear ducts a workout is this description of the death of the heroine in "The Widow and Her Son," a story in *The Sketch Book:* "She was too faint to rise—she attempted to extend her trembling hand—her lips moved as if she spoke, but no word was articulated—she looked down upon him with a smile of unutterable tenderness—and closed her eyes forever!" [1]

It is said that Washington Irving was "the first American to be known and recognized in England and on the Continent as a man of letters pure and simple." Since he fancied himself a sophisticated man of the world, he might not have been flattered by the "pure and simple" part.

[1] As this passage illustrates, there was a lot of dash about Irving's style.

IX

The Expanding Frontier

ABOUT the time the horizon was widening, the frontier was expanding. America was on the move, and Americans had to be quick about it, or they would be left behind as the rivers and mountains rushed past them.

James Fenimore Cooper

One of the writers most interested in the frontier was James Fenimore Cooper, who watched from his front porch in Cooperstown, New York, until it disappeared from sight in the west.[1] Not many know that he was born James Cooper and did not have a middle name until he was thirty-seven, but anyone who tries to get up a conversation about James Cooper, the novelist, will learn just how important the Fenimore is.

One day Cooper, after reading an English romance, boasted to his wife, "I could write a better book than that." If she had shrugged it off with "Of course you can, dear. Now turn off the light and come to bed," Cooper might have continued his happy career as the easygoing son of a wealthy country squire. But she blurted out, "Why don't you?" and in such a snide, skeptical tone that Cooper

---

[1] It was more than a coincidence that Cooper lived in a town named Cooperstown. His father, not known for modesty, founded the place.

shouted, "By G – –, I will!" [1] She could have kicked herself afterward, because for the next twenty years her husband sat at his desk from morning till night, without speaking to her, and the scratching of his quill almost drove her insane.

The hero of several of Cooper's novels is "Natty" Bumppo, called Leatherstocking because of the leather

Natty Bumppo

stockings which this fastidious dresser thought the height of style. He also clung to them (and they clung to him, especially in hot weather) because, unlike other stockings, they were never made unsightly by a run. Cooper's hero kept turning up in his various novels under such aliases as Deerslayer and Hawkeye, slaying deer and eyeing hawks but always the same dependable old Bumppo underneath. With his trusty rifle (never a trifle rusty) in hand and a spare canoe always parked in a nearby cave, he was a good man to have hiding behind the same tree with you.

Cooper's novels of the frontier are full of Indians of many tribes, such as Hurons (Bad Indians) and Delawares (Good Indians), Savages and Noble Savages. Anyone who has read *The Last of the Mohicans* will never forget

[1] Note how considerate it was of Cooper to say "G – –" in front of his wife.

Chingachgook (no relation to Gobbledygook) and his son Uncas, or the way people were always being aroused to danger by the breaking of a twig. Then there is that great scene where an evil Huron "sheathes his knife in the bosom of Cora," and his chief, the still more evil Magua, leaps upon Uncas and "passes his knife into his bosom three several times." Whether it was three times or several, it was enough. What with the killing of Cora's killer by Uncas and the killing of Uncas's killer by Hawkeye, hardly a bosom was left unperforated.

Time and again Cooper proved himself a master at depicting the vanishing Indian—one moment in clear view and the next, before you could draw a bead on him,[1] out of sight in the bushes.

Not all of Cooper's novels are about the wilderness. Some, like *The Pilot*, are sea stories, which he wrote after reading a sea story by Sir Walter Scott. "I can do better than that," he said. His wife managed to keep still this time, but it was no use. No question about it, Cooper had a competitive streak in him.

[1] Why you should want to draw a bead on an Indian, already weighted down by real beads, I fail to understand.

Depicting the vanishing Indian

X

William Cullen Bryant

BRYANT," says one scholar, "steadily declines to be classified in any group movement in our literature." Presumably this gentleman asked the poet, again and again, "How about the Transcendentalists?" "The Romanticists?" "The Graveyard School?" But Bryant's answer was always the same: "No." So we must give him a chapter all by himself.

An unusual thing about Bryant is that he wrote his best poem, "Thanatopsis," when he was seventeen. Since he lived until he was eighty-four, and, try as he might, could never do quite as well again, he is not to be blamed for becoming a little morbid. As a matter of fact he was morbid from an early age. In "Thanatopsis," as a teen-ager, he eagerly looked forward to the day when he would "mix forever with the elements" and be "a brother to th' insensible rock and to the sluggish clod." The only trouble with having a rock and a clod in the family, brothers under the soil, was the chance of being run down by a plowshare or tickled by a growing root. It was likely to be a little crowded down there.

Indeed, death had such a fascination for Bryant that when he picked up the morning paper he turned at once to the obituary column. "Lucky people," he muttered enviously. In addition to being a writer, Bryant was a lawyer, a newspaper editor, and a famous orator. What seems strange is that he never became a mortician.

Bryant's preoccupation with death was matched only by his love of nature, as seen in such poems as "To a Waterfowl" and "To the Fringed Gentian." These two poems have much in common, the titles of both, for instance, beginning with *To*. Bryant had a forthright way of speaking directly to a bird or a flower. "Whither," he asks the waterfowl, "thy solitary way?" Since it was December, the bird thought it obvious that it was heading south, and so disdained to answer. Besides, Bryant was holding something in his hand, and how was the waterfowl, "at that far height," to know it was a pen, not a pistol? In "The Yellow Violet" the poet says, "Sweet flower, I love, in forest

Communicating with nature

bare, to meet thee," and one gets a striking picture of Bryant, stark naked, running through the woods, hands outstretched, and the shrinking violet shrinking.

One of Bryant's most loved poems about a bird is "Robert of Lincoln," praising the merry bobolink. This is the lyric in which each of the eight stanzas has the wistful refrain, "Chee, chee, chee." Only a major poet would think of saying "Chee, chee, chee" eight times [1] in a single poem.

[1] Or "chee" twenty-four times.

Bryant's two consuming interests, death and nature, are joined in a poem entitled "The Death of the Flowers." When reading of the tragic demise of the violet, the aster, and the brier-rose, one finds it hard to remain unmoved. "Where are the flowers?" asks the poet. Then, before anyone gets any crazy notions, he answers:

Alas! they are all in their graves, the gentle race of flowers
Are lying in their lowly beds. . . .

At this point the reader is likely to choke up and, if no one is looking, shed a tear. Next Sunday he promises to go to a flower cemetery, and decorate all those little graves with people.

XI

The Transcendentalists

AFTER Irving, Cooper, and Bryant, the literary center of the United States moved from New York to New England. On Moving Day, roads were clogged with hundreds of poets, novelists, essayists, and editors, loaded down with the tools of their trade.[1]

The Transcendentalists were a group of New Englanders who looked upon themselves as mystics and were looked upon by others as queer. They formed a club, originally called the Aesthetic Club, or possibly Anaesthetic Club, where they sat around and talked about Immanuel Kant.[2] "I believe there was seldom an inclination to be silent," said one of the members. This is a Bostonian's way of saying that everybody talked at once.

One practical result of discussions at the Club was establishment of Brook Farm, a socialistic community where agriculture and the arts mingled, it being common practice to milk a cow with one hand while painting a landscape or writing a poem with the other. Mostly, however, unpleasant chores were assigned to a committee and forgotten, life being so beautiful that everyone was too busy looking at it to work. Despite emphasis on the individual, there

[1] Pens, erasers, paperweights, and rejection slips.
[2] "If Kant can't, nobody can," they were wont to say admiringly.

was belief in mutual helpfulness. It was, as Emerson said, "an attempt to lift others with themselves." The sight of a Brook farmer struggling to lift himself with one hand and a friend with the other sometimes startled passersby.

Ralph Waldo Emerson

The leader of the Transcendentalists was Ralph Waldo Emerson. Ralph (as few dared call him) came of a long line of Puritan ministers, which explains a great deal. He himself was a preacher for a while, and even after he left the pulpit continued preaching, as anyone knows who has read his essays.

Emerson lived most of his life in Boston and in Concord. In the latter he occupied a house that had been built for his grandfather and was therefore referred to as "the Old Man's." [1] It was there that Emerson wrote his book *Nature*, which is about nature. There too, during a heavy

---

[1] Mistakenly referred to today as the Old Manse.

rainstorm, he made his famous pronouncement: "Nature is not fixed but fluid."

A versatile writer, Emerson wrote both prose and poetry. It has been said that there are poetic passages in his prose and prosaic passages in his poetry. No doubt he did this on purpose, to confound his critics.[1] However, his poetry can easily be distinguished, even when it is not distinguished poetry, by such lines as:

> I like a church; I like a cowl;
> I love a prophet of the soul.

If you mispronounce either *cowl* or *soul*, but not both, it rhymes perfectly.

Many of Emerson's essays were first delivered as lectures. These lectures (for which he was well paid—see his essay "Compensation") took him all over the United States and to Europe. In England he was entertained by famous writers. One of them, George Eliot, jotted this somewhat cryptic entry in her diary: "He is the first *man* I have ever met." She was living at the time with George Henry Lewes, and it is a good thing she kept the key to her diary on a string around her neck.[2]

Emerson has been described as "a deep-seated genius," which is the kind of remark about a writer's physical appearance that a literary critic should never make. It would be kinder to say something about his Over-Soul, which might have been big and baggy but didn't show.[3]

[1] "Confound my critics!" Emerson often said.

[2] George Eliot, it should be noted, was *not* a man.

[3] Or did it? Emerson himself refers to the Over-Soul as "the lap of immense intelligence."

In his essays,[1] Emerson urges reliance on self, which he refers to as Self-Reliance. In fact self was so important to him that when he traveled in Europe he wrote in his journal, after a hard day's sightseeing, "Wherever we go, whatever we do, self is the sole subject we study and learn." Some think he might have saved all that money and stayed home.

Anyone who has difficulty understanding Emerson will be helped by the following explanation: "The Kantian tripartition supplied the epistemological terminology for Emersonian transcendentalism." Suddenly it all becomes clear.

Henry David Thoreau

The No. 2 Transcendentalist, whose number was up before Emerson's (he lived to be only forty-five), was

[1] Entitled, with Emerson's customary flair for the unusual, *Essays, First Series* and *Essays, Second Series*.

Henry David Thoreau.[1] Thoreau grew up in Concord, where his father was a manufacturer of lead pencils. Since the youth could have all the rejects that couldn't be sold, it is no wonder he became a writer.

Rather than earn money, it was Thoreau's idea to reduce his wants so that he would not need to buy anything. As he went around town preaching this ingenious idea, the shopkeepers of Concord hoped he would drop dead. Nor did his refusal to pay taxes endear him to local officials. Shuddering at the prospect of having a crank like Thoreau in the county jail, always demanding his special health-food diet, they paid his taxes and considered themselves fortunate.

Thoreau built himself a cabin on the shores of Walden Pond, near Concord, at a cost of $28.12½.[2] At least that

---

[1] At first his name was David Henry Thoreau, but apparently he got himself mixed up.

[2] Thoreau not only cut corners, he cut pennies.

Do-it-yourself cabin

is what he told the county tax assessor when he came to appraise the place. Thoreau was his own architect, carpenter, plasterer, and electrician, and he did without plumbing.[1]

Why Thoreau went to live alone at Walden, where he stayed two years and two months, he once explained as follows: "I wanted to live deep and suck out all the marrow of life." The picture of this rugged individualist crouched in a hole he had dug near his cabin, working away on a bone, is likely to linger for many a day.

Emerson, who enjoyed comfort, wrote of Thoreau somewhat irascibly: "I tell him a man was not made to live in a swamp, but a frog. If God meant him to live in a swamp, he would have made him a frog." Thoreau, who loved frogs just as he did ants and beetles, accepted this as a compliment and on summer evenings took to croaking softly.

Out of his experiences Thoreau wrote *Walden*, which hymns the pleasures of being alone with nature—away from newspapers, telephones, and Ralph Waldo Emerson. "If the bell rings, why should we run?" asks Thoreau. Callers who knocked on the door of his cabin often went away, thinking he was not home. Actually, he was getting out of his chair, but slowly.

It is probably unnecessary to say that Thoreau, preoccupied with eliminating what he called "superfluities," never married.[2]

---

[1] There were woods all around the place.

[2] "As for taking Henry's arm," said one of his friends, "I should as soon think of taking the arm of an elm tree." Thoreau was a lovable fellow, but there was something a little wooden about him.

Other Transcendentalists

Other Transcendentalists included Orestes Brownson, who, fortunately, was not on a first-name basis with many persons, and Bronson Alcott. Alcott founded Fruitlands, an experiment in vegetarian living, which broke up after a few months. One night at dinner, when the Fruitlanders were eating squash and turnip greens for the fourteenth time that week, the scent of roast beef drifted in from a neighboring farmhouse.

With the failure of Fruitlands, Alcott was in financial straits, but, being a man of high ideals, he refused to permit just anyone to support him. Almost the only person who passed his rigorous standards was his daughter, Louisa May Alcott, who had made a fortune with her *Little Women*, a sweet tearful saga of four sisters.[1]

There was also Margaret Fuller, whom the male Transcendentalists accepted as an intellectual equal. Fortunately for her, these eccentrics were more interested in brains than beauty. As editor of the Transcendentalist publication, the *Dial*, she displayed a blend of idealism and practicality by paying nothing to its contributors. Of course, the fact that the paid circulation of the *Dial* never exceeded 250 may have limited her funds.

---

[1] The term *sob sister* was first applied to Beth and her damp siblings.

XII

Edgar Allan Poe

UNLIKELY as it may seem, in view of his drinking, gambling, and opium-taking, Edgar Allan Poe was born in Boston. However, he spent most of his life in Richmond, Baltimore, and New York, where his gay habits caused fewer eyebrows to be lifted. The reason for Poe's being born in Boston was that his father and mother were actors,[1] and they happened to be playing there at the time.

Like James Fenimore Cooper, Edgar Allan Poe was born without a middle name.[2] The Allan was added later, making it possible for him to be distinguished from all the other Eddie Poes in the block.

Both of Edgar's parents died while playing in Richmond, and he was left an orphan at the tender age of two. What with his being an orphan and subsequently having trouble with his guardian, young Poe, with his high forehead and large, sad eyes, surely must have been Dickens' model for David Copperfield. Anyhow, he had a Difficult Youth.

Though he may not seem the type for a military man, his mustache being droopy instead of bristly, Poe served for a while in the Army. He enlisted under the name of

---

[1] He was born of "poor actor parents," says one biographer, but we prefer not to judge their acting ability.

[2] A fascinating parallel, often overlooked by superficial scholars.

Edgar A. Perry so that he would throw everyone off and yet be able to use his trunk with the initials E. A. P. on it. Then he briefly attended West Point, where he was court-martialed for misconduct—caught writing a poem while on guard duty. Had Poe graduated from West Point and lived until 1865 (when he would have been only fifty-six) instead of dying in 1849, he might have risen high in the Union Army and lost the war.[1]

To keep body and soul together, Poe worked madly as an editor, critic, poet, and short-story writer. There were

Edgar Allan Poe

several rules about writing poetry which Poe admired and followed faithfully, since they were his own. One was that a poem should be about the death of a beautiful woman. Since Poe's women, especially those with names like Lenore and Ulalume, were usually sickening by the second stanza, they were dead before there was time to summon a physician. Poe's own wife, whom he married when she was thirteen, hoping she would last a while, made it only to twenty-six.

[1] It is said that Poe "drank to excess." We can just see him, glass lifted, crying "To Excess!"

Sickening women
60

Another rule, and probably the most popular with Poe's readers, was that a poem should be short enough to be read at one sitting. Whether the chair should be hard, over-stuffed, or a rocker, Poe does not specify. "The Raven" may be a little lengthy for the fidgety reader, though it can be shortened materially by skipping the word *Nevermore* after the first few stanzas.[1]

In Poe's stories someone is always hiding a body or burying the victim alive. Any well-appointed home, such as that of Roderick Usher in "The Fall of the House of Usher," is as sure to have a vault or a catacomb as a guest

bedroom or a second bath, and there is always a spare coffin in the hall closet. Sometimes, as in "The Cask of Amontillado," the murderer carries a trowel and, happily coming upon some building stone and a supply of freshly mixed mortar, can seal up an erstwhile friend, dead or alive, in a jiffy.

One of the peculiar things about the people who die and are securely entombed in Poe's stories is that you can never be sure they will stay dead, or stay put. That creaking sound may be a coffin lid opening, and that *scrape, scrape* on the stone may be the recently deceased. To a murderer, this kind of thing can be mighty discouraging.

[1] Similarly, omit the word *bells* in "The Bells" and see how short the poem becomes.

Poe is usually considered gloomy and humorless. But we must not overlook a delightful scene in "The Tell-Tale Heart." The murderer having cut off the head, arms, and legs of his victim preparatory to burying him under the floor, you would suppose the place might be a mite messy. But no. As Poe laughingly tells us, "There was nothing to wash out—no stain of any kind—no blood-spot whatever. I had been too wary for that. A tub had caught it all—ha! ha!" The reader, relieved, joins the guffawing.

In his relentless search for beauty, Poe wrote about cobwebs, corpses, and worms. There is probably no more heartfelt tribute to a worm than his reference, in one of his poems, to "the Conqueror Worm," with its "vermin fangs in human gore imbued," slurping away. As for the pit in "The Pit and the Pendulum," it is as pitiful as you will find in English or American literature. Then there is the ruined building in "The Fall of the House of Usher," where "minute fungi overspread the whole exterior, hanging in a fine tangled web-work from the eaves." This is matched only by the ancient abbey in "Ligeia," with its "verdant decay." Poe liked his women young and his houses old, perhaps for contrast.

To get the utmost pleasure from the stories and poems of Poe, you should read them at midnight in some ghoul-haunted woodland when the leaves are withering and sere. It will help, too, if this is near a dark tarn, at the edge of which is a mouldering plinth.[1] Then, if a bat suddenly flies past, startled out of a tomb by the tolling of rusty bells, you will understand why Poe took to drink.

[1] It need not be a plinth if, like the present writer, you do not know what a plinth is, but it should be mouldering—definitely.

XIII

Nathaniel Hawthorne

ALMOST as gloomy as Poe was Nathaniel Hawthorne.[1] Hawthorne's moody character is said to have been caused by having Puritanism in his veins, which must be almost as bad as Tired Blood. One of Hawthorne's ancestors had been a witch-burner, but he contented himself with burning manuscripts of stories he could not sell. An-

Provided with warmth

other way Hawthorne differed from his forebears was that they spelled the name Hathorne. He put in the *w* while he was in college, tired of being called "Hat horn" and "Ha! Thorne."

[1] Hawthorne, however, was sober, which was not always true of Poe.

Hawthorne spent most of his life in Salem. There, he tells us, his ancestors lived and died and "mingled their earthly substance with the soil." Until he was fifty, he never got farther away from New England than Niagara Falls, and what he saw going on there, with honeymooners all about, he could hardly wait to recount to the good people back home.

For fourteen years, Hawthorne hid away in a solitary chamber under the eaves in the family home in Salem. Emerging at last, "I relied for support on my pen," he tells us, no doubt feeling weak.

Hawthorne did not marry until he was thirty-seven, when he took as his bride Sophia Peabody, a Transcendentalist who shared his love.[1] She was a blue-stocking, as Hawthorne noticed once when he shyly glanced at her legs. It is no wonder they named their first child Una, after the heroine of the first book of *The Faerie Queene*. Had it been a son, the lad would probably have been called Red Cross Knight, or R. C. K. Hawthorne. Hawthorne's favorite story, it should be noted, was *Pilgrim's Progress*, and he kept reading over and over the part about the Slough of Despond. "I wish I had thought of that," he sighed.

Hawthorne, whose mother lived in genteel poverty (the best kind) after the death of her husband, had a hard time making a living with his pen.[2] He was forced into such jobs as a weigher at the Boston Custom House and United States Consul at Liverpool, where he was astonished to find

[1] Of books.
[2] Bent as it was from supporting him.

that natives of that city are called Liverpudlians.[1] He also spent a short time at Brook Farm, where, after carefully examining his credentials, the authorities assigned him to important duties in the potato patch and the manure pile.[2]

Among Hawthorne's works are *Twice-Told Tales*, in which each tale is told twice for the sake of readers who do not get it the first time, *The House of the Seven Gables* (Mr. and Mrs. and their five little ones), and *The Scarlet Letter*, which is on most high school reading lists in the hope that girls will get the idea before it is too late.

The Scarlet Letter is the story of a young woman who commits adultery with her minister and has an illegitimate

With her minister

child. Before the modern reader asks "So what?" let it be pointed out that this was in Puritan New England, when this sort of thing was still frowned upon. The story has been called a triangle, doubtless with reference to the

[1] The *pool* changes to *puddle* when it is moved from a place to a person.

[2] This is the truth, once again proving that truth is stranger than biography.

woman, the woman's husband, and the preacher, but this fails to take into account the illegitimate child, who makes it a rectangle. It is full of symbolism, which means that everything stands for something—except the young woman's husband, who won't stand for what has been going on behind his back. One's sympathies are with the adulteress, Hester Prynne, because she has to go around in a blouse with a big red letter *A* on it. Before the book ends, there is trouble aplenty, and the moral is clear for young women: keep away from church.

In the short story "The Minister's Black Veil," the clergyman wears a black veil over his face all his life, and not just to keep out mosquitoes. When he preaches, his congregation is more than a little upset. "Such was the effect of this simple piece of crape," writes Hawthorne, "that more than one woman of delicate nerves was forced to leave the meeting-house." The minister undoubtedly found it hard to shave, reaching up under the veil.

In *The Marble Faun*, a novel set in Italy, where almost anything can happen, Hawthorne tells of an artist with pointed ears who pushes a man over a cliff to please his girl friend, and gets nothing out of it but a prison sentence. All of this, it is clear,[1] shows Hawthorne's obsession with evil and guilt. No doubt about it: people are Bad.

Hawthorne was against sin. Without it, though, he would never have become a great author.

[1] At least to scholars who have become full professors by explaining Hawthorne's symbolism.

XIV

American Poetry
Comes of Age

IN the mid-nineteenth century, American poetry came of age. Since more than two hundred years had passed since the *Bay Psalm Book*, this is another instance of slow maturation. Even then, traces of childishness lingered.

Henry Wadsworth Longfellow

That Longfellow was somewhat exceptional is evident in a letter he wrote his father while a student at Bowdoin College. "I most eagerly aspire after future eminence in literature," he declared, without a single mention of needing money or having gotten into a scrape with a chorus girl. He was a classmate of Hawthorne's at Bowdoin, a class that contributed more to the literary magazine than to the football team.

Longfellow became a full professor at Bowdoin when he was twenty-two, at $800 a year. This might seem a small salary today, but it was ample to meet Longfellow's needs: pen, paper, three meals a week, and occasionally a fresh antimacassar. After a sojourn in Europe, where he saturated himself in German romantic poetry, apparently sitting in vats of the stuff, he took a professorship at Harvard. The move from Bowdoin he explained by saying he wished "to tread a stage on which I can take longer strides." He was a restless lecturer, always pacing about, and at Bowdoin was often in danger of falling into the orchestra pit.

Always pacing about

Despite his success as a teacher at Harvard, "his heart was elsewhere." Being in one place and having your heart in another is usually fatal for anyone but a poet.[1] Longfellow put up with this from 1836 to 1854, when he resigned his professorship on the advice of a heart specialist. All the while, living in Craigie House in Cambridge, he was writing poetry. A contemporary describes him as "sitting by the fireside writing verse on his knee with his eyes closed." It is assumed that he wrote only his shorter lyrics on his knee, saving his thigh and larger areas for such poems as *Evangeline* and *Hiawatha*. And why did he keep

[1] See the astonishing case of Robert Burns. "My heart's in the Highlands," he said, "a-chasing the deer." You can imagine how frightened the deer was, glancing back over its shoulder at this gruesome pursuer.

68

his eyes closed? No doubt so he would not have to read what he had just written.

Longfellow's poetry was popular from the start and sold so well that he became the first American [1] to make a living as a poet. *The Courtship of Miles Standish* [2] sold 25,000 copies in a single week, a rate that has been equaled only by such literary works as *Fannie Farmer's Cookbook*.

Hiawatha, which popularized Trochaic Tetrameters,[3] tells of the love of Hiawatha for Minnehaha. Hiawatha showed admirable restraint in not sometimes saying Minnehahahaha and winding up with a bad case of hysterics. It is in *Hiawatha*, by the way, that one finds those notable lines,

> Oh the long and dreary Winter!
> Oh the cold and cruel Winter!

in which Longfellow proves his lyric mastery by saying the

[1] And possibly the last.

[2] Someone may yet write a poem entitled *The Courtship of Henry Wadsworth Longfellow*, describing Longfellow's seven-year effort to win his second wife, a courtship of truly epic proportions.

[3] A metrical form, not a cough drop.

Hiawatha—Mighty hunter woos Minnehaha

69

same thing twice but with just enough variation to get away with it.

Who does not know the opening line of many of Longfellow's poems? Before answering this question, here is another. Who knows the rest of the poem? Take "The shades of night were falling fast," which obviously refers to the fact that it was night, and people were hurrying to pull down their shades. To help those who have trouble getting any further, we repeat this memorable line and suggest one to follow which, if not Longfellow's, will serve the purpose:

> The shades of night were falling fast,
> And Peeping Toms were foiled at last.

Similarly we offer these famous first lines of Longfellow's, each with an infamous second line:

> Tell me not, in mournful numbers,
> The price you paid for two cucumbers.

> Listen, my children, and you shall hear
> The gurgling sound as I down my beer.

> Under a spreading chestnut-tree
> Were rusty cans and such debris.

> I shot an arrow into the air. . . .
> It still may fall some day—beware!

Longfellow is known for his profound philosophical observations, such as "Life is real! Life is earnest!" [1] and "Into each life some rain must fall," a thought which came to him one day when caught in a downpour without his rubbers and umbrella. Anyone in a like situation will find

---

[1] The exclamation points are his, not mine.

quoting this line a great help, provided he has a dry sense of humor.

When Longfellow died, the English hid his bust in Poets' Corner.

John Greenleaf Whittier

As a youth on a New England farm, Whittier was a barefoot boy with cheek of tan, though he eventually got a pair of shoes and lost some of his cheek. When he was fourteen, "a volume of Burns's poetry fell into his hands," which was a stroke of good luck in that it did not fall on his head.

Whittier was a "fighting Quaker," [1] gritting his teeth and clenching his fists whenever he saw a Social Injustice. At the very thought of slavery, Whittier would go into a frenzy and take violent action, writing a poem.

[1] The same as a "militant pacifist."

Militant pacifist

When he was not describing "slavery's hateful hell," he was writing about something more to his liking: meadows rich with corn, meadows sweet with hay, and meadows full of simple creatures like Maud Muller. It was of Maud Muller, by the bye, that Whittier wrote probably the sexiest lines in any of his poetry, pruriently referring to her graceful ankles and long-lashed hazel eyes. This was in 1854, at the height of the Victorian period, and it is a wonder the poem was not banned for its anatomical frankness.

The most famous of Whittier's works is *Snow-Bound*. Whittier wrote this poem, as most others, in a simple, direct way, unaware of the importance of symbolism and hidden meanings which might have made him a Great Poet or at least the subject of doctoral dissertations. Nor did it occur to him to employ such exciting typographical devices as contributed to the fame of E. E. Cummings, born two years after Whittier's death. Otherwise he might have written the opening lines of *Snow Bound* in some such fashion as this:

> th
> e sun
> that briefdecemberday
> rose
> chee
> rless
> over hills
> of gra
> y

But Whittier stuck to simple themes and saw nothing wrong with old-fashioned capitals, commas, and periods. Moreover, he was fond of nature, as befits a man whose middle name was Greenleaf, and unashamed of homely toil among homely people. We leave Whittier knee-deep in lilies and wood-grapes, happy with "the wild bee's morning chase." Despite dyspepsia and migraine headaches, he was able to run over hill and dale, just out of stinger range, until the bee dropped exhausted on the new-mown sward. Since he never married, Whittier had plenty of time for this sort of wholesome sport, and it kept him out in the fresh air.

Oliver Wendell Holmes

Oliver Wendell Holmes was a poet, essayist, novelist, doctor, and professor of anatomy. Some think he was also an Associate Justice of the Supreme Court.[1] He was a New England Brahmin, and is not to be confused with an East Indian Brahman, which has short horns and a large hump over the shoulders.[2]

Among Holmes's works are *The Deacon's Masterpiece*,[3] *The Chambered Nautilus*, and *The Contagiousness of Puerperal Fever*. Out of his experience with surgery came *Old Ironsides*, about a patient on whom he broke several expensive scalpels before making an incision. Of Dr. Holmes's medical career, it might be said that he went into teaching because patients asked to see his medical certificate before permitting him to feel their pulse. This may have been

[1] That was his son, who is thought by some to have been a poet, essayist, novelist, doctor, and professor of anatomy.

[2] Also known, by cattle fanciers, as a zebu.

[3] Or *The Wonderful "One-Hoss Shay,"* an interesting instance of the subtitle being better known than the title.

Holmes was on the short side

because Dr. Holmes was only five feet three and weighed less than his little black bag full of pills and tongue depressors. Also, he turned deathly pale at the sight of blood.

Holmes was such a witty conversationalist that he could hardly wait to get the family together in the morning, though their eyes were hardly open. These early morning monologues were gathered into such volumes as *The Autocrat of the Breakfast Table*, *The Professor at the Breakfast Table*, and *The Poet at the Breakfast Table*. No wonder Holmes was small and thin, since he never stopped talking long enough to eat.

The intricacy and imagery of Holmes's poetry have been much admired, and we cite as examples such beautiful lines as these, from *The Last Leaf:*

> I saw him once before,
> As he passed by the door,

and

74

> But now he walks the streets
> And he looks at all he meets.

This is the kind of poetry that sent critics digging deep beneath the surface for meaning. There's certainly none on the surface.

The playfulness of Holmes is indicated by the opening lines of *My Aunt:*

> My aunt! my dear unmarried aunt!
> Long years have o'er her flown;
> Yet still she strains the aching clasp
> That binds her virgin zone.

Some readers have been disappointed, as they read on, to discover that Holmes was not referring to a chastity belt but to a corset.

However Holmes was not all fun and frivolity. Returning to *The Last Leaf*, we are sobered by the pathetic lines:

> My grandmamma has said—
> Poor old lady, she is dead. . . .

American poetry was, truly, coming of age. And Holmes's grandmamma, poor old lady, didn't live to see it.

James Russell Lowell

James Russell Lowell, another New England poet, is said to have had "the deep thoughtfulness of Emerson, the technical skill of Longfellow, the ready wit of Holmes, and the pastoral quality of Whittier." No wonder he needed few characteristics of his own. However, in "The Courtin'" in *The Biglow Papers* the feller manages, by crickey, to sound like himself:

He was six foot o' man, A 1,[1]
Clear grit an' human natur',
None couldn't quicker pitch a ton
Nor dror a furrer straighter.

As a Harvard graduate and editor of the *Atlantic Monthly*, it must have been difficult for Lowell to write like an illiterate oaf, but he succeeded. He also succeeded Longfellow as Professor of Modern Languages at Harvard, perhaps because he had invented a modern language of his own.

Succeeded Longfellow

Lowell was not only a poet but also a critic, and in *A Fable for Critics* he made it plain what was wrong with Emerson, Bryant, Poe, Cooper, and others. He even criticized James Russell Lowell, to show he was a good sport, but none too harshly. In rhymes such as "change a line" and "Evangeline," "dwelt on" and "Felton," and "plea for it" and "fee for it" he may well have influenced Ogden Nash.

When his wife died, Lowell stopped writing poetry. Many think he had done it, all those years, just to annoy her.

[1] His draft status, no doubt.

XV

Herman Melville

Herman MELVILLE made Americans conscious of the South Pacific and paved the way for James A. Michener. His first experience with the sea came as a young man of twenty, when he shipped before the mast to England. The mast arrived a week later.

Two years passed,[1] and then he went on a whaling voyage to the Pacific, out of which came *Typee*. The full title of this novel is *Typee: A Peep at Polynesian Life*. Herman peeped especially at Fayaway, a beautiful native maiden with whom he was forced by a curious tribal custom to live as man and wife without benefit of clergy. (Actually it is hard to see how any clergy could have benefited.) He finally fled the natives when he discovered where their meat supply came from and heard them talking about New York cuts. A New Yorker himself, he didn't like the way his hosts kept feeling his ribs.

Melville's great work is, of course, *Moby Dick*, about a mad captain [2] and his search for the great white whale that had carried off his leg. Though Captain Ahab could never hope to get his leg back intact, and would have no

[1] It took that long for him to forget what it was like to be seasick.
[2] He was doubly mad, being both crazy and angry.

use for it, except maybe to hang over the mantel, he pursues Moby Dick relentlessly. With remarkable restraint, the author keeps one of his two chief characters, the whale after whom the book is named, out of the novel until Chapter CXXXIII.

The reader of this classic of the sea will learn a great deal about the different kinds of whales, the history of whaling, and how to get the oil out of a whale,[1] picking up many Interesting Facts not usually found in a novel. Moby Dick is thought by some to represent Evil, and when the whale finally overcomes his pursuer, Captain Ahab, the reader can let out a sigh of relief, knowing that once more Evil has triumphed.

Few works have been so subject to interpretation. There are those who see *Moby Dick* as an allegory symbolizing the struggle between man and nature. Others, however, find it a thinly veiled epic of seasickness. In a brilliant piece of scholarship, one promising young researcher has discovered Internal Evidence that the name Ahab spelled backward is Baha. Baba is the noise a sheep makes . . . Ahab was a black sheep chasing a white whale . . . his wooden leg was a you-know-what symbol . . . and the whole thing adds up to miscegenation on the briny deep.

From time to time there has been a Melville revival, but it seems generally agreed that Captain Ahab is gone for good.

[1] It isn't easy. You don't just pull a plug.

XVI

Civil War Writers

TWO writers concerned with the Civil War were Harriet Beecher Stowe and Abraham Lincoln. Though both were against slavery, they had little else in common. Only one, for instance, wore a beard and a stovepipe hat.

Mrs. Stowe played a rather important part in the Civil

Two Civil War writers

War. She caused it. Almost single-handed [1] she inflamed the North with her *Uncle Tom's Cabin*, a book about slavery in which sentimentality and horror are so intermingled

[1] What she might have done with both hands is interesting to contemplate.

that many critics have found it horribly sentimental. It is hard to forget Uncle Tom, a kindly old fellow who could never understand why his master was always beating him. It is also hard to forget Eliza, the runaway slave, jumping from ice cake to ice cake [1] with her young child in her arms, and thus managing to cross the Ohio River without taking the ferry. And who can forget Little Eva or Topsy or Simon Legree, especially Legree, the brutal plantation owner who kept himself fit by using Uncle Tom as a punching bag? The book is, in short, full of Unforgettable Characters and Memorable Scenes, and has been responsible for many a nightmare.

In *Uncle Tom's Cabin,* Mrs. Stowe achieved what had been thought impossible—she made slavery seem almost as bad as it really was.

Abraham Lincoln is probably better known as a President than as a writer. Nonetheless his Gettysburg Address and his Second Inaugural are masterpieces of compression, showing clearly that Lincoln was not being paid by the word. The Gettysburg Address is one of the few addresses written on the back of an envelope, most being written on the front. And it was in his Second Inaugural Address that he made his famous reference to croquet, "With mallets toward none."

Despite his tendency to succinctness, Lincoln could occasionally be wordy, as he was when he said "four score and seven" instead of "eighty-seven." Though he was generally optimistic, there is a note of helplessness in "we cannot dedicate, we cannot consecrate, we cannot hallow," and for a moment one knows not which way to turn. Almost

---

[1] Each cake covered with frosting.

as vigorous an outdoorsman as Hemingway, Lincoln was fond of splitting rails. He also used the language of sports, especially boxing, as when he insisted that "a right makes might," though he also had a healthy respect for a left uppercut.

If Lincoln's writings are brief, this is compensated for by the length of the books about him. See, for example, Carl Sandburg's six-volume biography, in which nothing unimportant is omitted.

XVII

Walt Whitman

MANY questions have been raised about Walt Whitman. One, which we are happy to be able to answer, is: Was his first name Walt or was it really Walter? It was Walter.[1] Whitman's father, Walter, named his first three sons after three great Americans, George Washington, Thomas Jefferson, and Andrew Jackson. Upon the arrival of the fourth, the only other great American he could think of was himself.

As young Walt [2] intimates in "Out of the Cradle Endlessly Rocking," he thought his parents were going to treat him like a baby forever. But at long last he left home. One of the first places he went to, as he tells us in *Specimen Days,* was Coney Island, "at that time a long, bare unfrequented shore, which I had all to myself, and where I loved, after bathing, to race up and down the hard sand, and declaim Homer or Shakespeare to the surf and seagulls by the hour." How amazed Walt would be to see Coney Island today, and how amazed the crowds at Coney Island, on a Sunday, would be to see Walt racing down the beach declaiming Homer or Shakespeare to the seagulls.

[1] But just try referring to the American poet Walter Whitman and see the looks you get.

[2] "Junior" Whitman somehow sounds like a small box of candy.

During the Civil War, Whitman was a male nurse in a Washington hospital. To wounded soldiers, who had dreamt about the beautiful nurses who would care for them during their recuperation, Walt was something of a disappointment. Some of them even refused to let him take their pulse.

If Whitman at times seems a little confused about his sex, there is also evidence that he was actually a hairy-chested type. See, for example, the manly poem entitled "Scented Herbage of My Breast." There is no doubt, however, that he was a little odd, among other things being a student of phrenology and keeping a chart of his bumps. He had, after all, taken some pretty hard knocks.

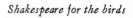

Shakespeare for the birds

83

Whitman's most famous book of poems was *Leaves of Grass*. A man of many parts,[1] he was not only his own book designer and publisher, but also wrote some of the most favorable reviews. Despite all his efforts, contemporary reactions to *Leaves* was disappointing. For instance Whittier, to whom he gave a copy, threw it into the fire. Some think the Quaker poet feared for the morals of the young people in the family; others, who have read *Snow-Bound*, believe it must have been a cold night and he was short of firewood. At any rate, Whitman had to give most of the copies away, and is credited with originating free verse.[2]

Among the poems in *Leaves of Grass* is "Song of Myself." It held up publication of the book for several days, until the printer could get a new supply of type, having run out of the letter *I*. Whitman's gusto, his enjoyment of life,

[1] All of which he celebrated in "Song of Myself."
[2] Later editions of the book sold very well, people by this time realizing that some of Whitman's poems were immoral.

Song of myself

is most marked in "Song of the Open Road," a poem addressed to a friend named Allons. "Allons!" he says, "come travel with me," and "Allons! the road is before us." Once out on the highway, he likes himself more than ever:

> I am larger, better than I thought,
> I did not know I held so much goodness.

But he is afraid that there isn't enough of him to go around, so he writes; "I will scatter myself among men and women as I go."

Whitman tried to persuade himself that he was an average man, but all the time there lurked within him the suspicion that he might be a little out of the ordinary. To avoid notice, he wore a big, floppy hat and, we are told, "rough clothing" (possibly tweeds). He is supposed to have worn no tie, affecting a Byronic open collar, though not even his closest friends dared to lift his beard and look. By the time he was eighteen he had begun to turn gray. In later life he was good and gray, and therefore known as the Good and Gray Poet.

In our exhaustive [1] reading of critical works on Whitman, nothing has struck us so forcibly as this sentence: "He attempted to embrace the whole of America—an impossible task for a poet." It would seem difficult for anyone, poet or not, unless he had very long arms indeed. Another interesting critical comment is this: "While one of his feet is planted solidly in the midst of the romantic movement in America, the other is advanced far in the direction of twentieth-century modernity."

Though we are loath to leave Walt Whitman in this awkward position, we must hurry on.

[1] We tire easily.

XVIII

Regional Writers

IN the latter half of the nineteenth century there were a number of regional or local-color writers. A local-color writer is not the same as an off-color writer, except occasionally. Some of these writers wrote in a local dialect, which everyone thought hilarious except the printer. An example is Henry Wheeler Shaw, whose spelling was so bad that his own name came out Josh Billings. Writing of mules, in his "Essa on the Muel," he says, "The only wa tu keep them in a paster, is tu turn them into a medder jineing, and let them jump in." There is something much funnier about "medder jineing" than "meadow adjoining." But if you want a real howler, try "Eri kanawl." Once you recognize this as "Erie Canal," you will be in stitches.

If you have finished laughing and have regained your composure, let us now turn to more serious literature.

Bret Harte

One of the writers of the West was Bret Harte. He was born in the East, but with that name he realized he had to move to California. His best-known stories are "The Outcasts of Poker Flat" and "The Luck of Roaring Camp," in

Bret Harte

both of which he proves that beneath a rough exterior there is often a heart of gold. This may explain why more than one grizzled miner was stabbed in the chest by a prospector's pick.

In "The Outcasts of Poker Flat," a work undoubtedly influenced by Whittier's *Snow-Bound,* some outcasts are snowed to death in an isolated cabin. One who gets away is a young fellow known as the Innocent, who goes for help on a pair of snowshoes "fashioned from the old pack saddle." [1] Another, John Oakhurst, a gambler, leaves the cabin and shoots himself rather than die of the cold. Bret Harte's characteristic tenderness is illustrated by the scene in which the Innocent kisses his fiancée, Piney, before going for help on the homemade snowshoes. "They unaffectedly exchanged a kiss," writes our author, "so honest and sincere that it might have been heard above the swaying pines." What a pity the lovers did not think to summon rescuers with a few more of those resounding smacks.

Joaquin Miller

Another writer of the West was Joaquin (Walk-een) Miller, who became famous as the American author whose

[1] Try it.

first name was most often mispronounced.[1] Miller thought of himself as the Byron of Oregon, and there are striking similarities. Both poets, for instance, ran off and left their wives.

His most famous poem is "Columbus," in which the first mate, hoarding his dwindling store of vowels, refers to Columbus as "Brave Adm'r'l," and Columbus, urged to say something, can think only of "Sail on! sail on! and

"Sail on! Sail on!"

on!" "Columbus" has been recited by millions of American schoolchildren to audiences consisting mostly of friends and relatives.

Few poets have liked "like" as much as Joaquin Miller. Describing an Indian chieftain in "The Last Taschastas," he says:

> His eye was like the lightning's wing,
> His voice was like a rushing flood. . . .
> His breast was like a gate of brass,
> His brow was like a gather'd storm.

[1] His first name was originally Cincinnatus, which was none too easy to roll off the tongue after a few drinks in the Deadeye Saloon.

It was in "Kit Carson's Ride," however, that he achieved his ultimate goal of four similes in two lines:

> While his eyes were like flame, his face like a shroud,
> His form like a king, and his beard like a cloud.

Joaquin Miller died in 1913, and we shall never see his "like" again.

Joel Chandler Harris

Local-color writers of the South included Sidney Lanier, George Washington Cable,[1] and Joel Chandler Harris. Because of his use of Negro dialect, Harris may be thought of not as a local-color writer but as a colored local writer. His stories are told by Uncle Remus and concern Brer Rabbit and Brer Fox.[2] Brer Fox was forever trying to get the better of Brer Rabbit, but Brer Rabbit was always too

[1] This always reminds us, somehow, of George Washington Bridge, no relation.

[2] Also Brer Wolf, Brer B'ar, Brer Buzzard, and many another who hung around the old Brer Patch.

Brer Harris and friends

smart for him. Once, for instance, Brer Fox invited Brer Rabbit to dinner, but when Brer Rabbit got to Brer Fox's house he could tell at a glance, from de dishpan w'at wuz settin' on de table en de kyarvin' knife close by dat Brer Fox wuz fixin' fur to 'vour him. How Brer Rabbit got out of this desperate situation we would not reveal for the world. Y'all jes haster read it fur y'self.

Brer Harris learned the Negro dialect from listening to animals talk on a Georgia plantation. Bimeby de reader hisself gets ter talkin' 'zackly like all de res' er um. Bless grashus! ain't nothin' much you kin do 'bout it, less'n you butts yo' head 'gin de do' jam'.

James Whitcomb Riley

James Whitcomb Riley, or The Hoosier Poet, lived in Indiana, the longtime home of the Rileys and the Hoosiers. His best-loved poems are "The Old Swimmin'-Hole," "When the Frost Is on the Punkin," and "Little Orphant Annie." He brings nostalgic tears to your eyes with his account of how he ust to have lots o' fun at the old swimmin'-hole where the bullrushes growed and his shadder ust to smile up at him. And you can just hear the buzzin' of the bees and the hummin' of the birds and the clackin' of the hens when he tells how a feller feels along about the time the frost is on the punkin and the fodder's in the shock.[1]

If you skeer easily, though, you had better not read "Little Orphant Annie" in bed at night, unless you can

---

[1] The shock is such that it usually kills the fodder, which turns brown. For how it feels to be fodderless, see Little Orphant Annie.

James Whitcomb Riley

read with the kivvers over your head. As Riley says, "The Gobble-uns 'll git you

> Ef you
> Don't
> Watch
> Out!"

What the Gobble-uns will do to you after they git you, he does not say, but they will probably gobble you up.[1]

[1] Or gobble you down. Or gobbledygook.

XIX

Mark Twain

MARK TWAIN, familiarly known as Samuel Langhorne Clemens, grew up in what is called the Huckleberry Finn House in Hannibal, Missouri, not to be confused with the Mickey Finn House, a bar in downtown Hannibal. He had little schooling, but acquired his literary style while working for newspapers and piloting a river boat, the latter experience adding to the richness of his vocabulary.

Few are aware of the part he played in the Civil War. A cavalryman in the Confederate Army, he kept riding west and wound up in Nevada, where he became so engrossed with prospecting for silver and writing for newspapers that he forgot all about the war. Four years later, when he remembered, it was over. "Shucks," he said, cheated out of all that glory and the chance of being killed.

If, however, any of his varied experiences can be said to have trained him for a career as a humorist and teller of tall tales, it was probably his employment for a time in Washington, where he was the secretary of a Senator.

Sam Clemens made a name for himself [1] with his story about "The Celebrated Jumping Frog of Calaveras County." He also made a name for the frog—Dan'l.

---

[1] That is, Mark Twain. He got the idea from the cry of riverboat men. Why they cried when they said "Mark Twain" is too complicated to go into here.

Made a name for himself

Shortly afterward he traveled to the Mediterranean. His letters home resulted in his first book, *The Innocents Abroad*,[1] and he was immediately recognized as a man of letters. It was on this trip that he fell in love with a picture of Olivia Langdon, whom he married as soon as he made sure that her photograph had not been unduly touched up. Miss Langdon was of a wealthy, pious family, and after their marriage she tried to make a gentleman of her husband. Happily, she was not successful.

Mark Twain is a major American writer. This is evident from the fact that his writings are divided into three categories. One of his works which is in a class by itself, and sometimes in a room by itself, is *1601: Conversation as It Was by the Fireside in the Time of the Tudors*. It is full of Elizabethan language,[2] some of it by Elizabeth herself, conversing with Sir Walter Raleigh, Ben Jonson, Shakespeare, and other immorals. Being Elizabethan rather than modern, it is not dirty but earthy, an important

[1] A man is said to have gone into a bookstore and asked for *The Innocent Broad*.

[2] A euphemism for "four-letter words."

distinction. Many of Mark Twain's friends considered it coarse and vulgar and asked for extra copies.

Other books by Mark Twain include *Tom Sawyer,* in which Huckleberry Finn is a character, and *Huckleberry Finn,* in which Tom Sawyer is a character. Of all the memorable episodes in *Tom Sawyer,* including a murder by Injun Joe in a cemetery and getting lost in a cave and finding a chest full of money, nothing is so memorable as the whitewashing incident. Tom makes whitewashing a fence so appealing that other boys pay him for the privilege. As those who have tried this since have discovered, too many other boys have read *Tom Sawyer.*

What one most remembers about *Huckleberry Finn* is Huck's voyage down the Mississippi with Jim, a runaway Negro slave, and the Duke and the King, a couple of con men. As Huck says, "There warn't no home like a raft. Other places do seem so cramped up and smothery, but a raft don't. You feel mighty free and easy and comfortable on a raft." Huck, who was always sneaking off to smoke in the woods or go fishing, never stayed in school long enough to learn grammar and how to avoid repetition. By proving how well he could get along without schooling, he set American education back fifty years.

Among Mark Twain's nonfiction works is *Life on the Mississippi,* in which he tells of becoming a cub pilot. Piloting a steamboat down the Mississippi in the dead of night with no landmarks to observe and only deep blackness all around was an eerie experience, as eerie as the Erie.

Mention should also be made of *The Prince and the Pauper, Roughing It,* and *A Connecticut Yankee in King Arthur's Court.*[1]

In his later years Mark Twain, who had created such characters as Huckleberry Finn and Pudd'nhead Wilson, himself became a character, wearing a white linen suit even in the dead of winter. He was always smoking a cigar, which he called a "segar," or a pipe, which he called a pipe.

Since his death there have been many impersonations of Mark Twain, but no one has ever impersonated Mark Twain as well as Samuel Clemens.

[1] An interesting bit of dialogue:
"You might also mention 'The Man That Corrupted Hadleyburg.' "
"Thanks."
"Don't mention it."

Impersonations of Mark Twain

XX

Emily Dickinson

EMILY DICKINSON is indubitably the greatest woman poet in American literature.[1] Some critics rank her with Elizabeth Barrett Browning, while others say she is worthy of being mentioned in the same breath with Sappho, Christina Rossetti, and Edith Sitwell. Persons considering such a mention should take a deep breath.

When she was a young woman, Miss Dickinson withdrew from society and told everyone she was not at home, when she was. In fact for the last fifteen years of her life she never left her father's house in Amherst, Massachusetts, except to go into the garden. It was during this period, too, that she wore only white,[2] and it is no wonder her family complained about the laundry bills. "At least stop kneeling in the mud when you cultivate your hollyhocks," they begged her.

There has been much speculation about why Emily became a recluse. Some say she had an unfortunate love affair with a clergyman. It was unfortunate because this particular clergyman was married. In this connection, scholars have gone to great lengths to find references to clergymen

---

[1] This is the first time the word *indubitably* has been used in this book. That it has been held back until now will give some idea of the author's powers of restraint.

[2] The only thing she had in common with Mark Twain.

in her poems. In their search for allusions to a man of the cloth, especially a defrocked or defrosted minister, they have noted Miss Dickinson's fondness for the color black, have counted the number of times she has mentioned such suggestive words as *man,* and have multiplied by two to allow for wind resistance, drift, and pages stuck together.

On the other hand, her sticking close to the house may have been prompted by her rather domineering father. He was a trustee of Amherst College, a local college for men, and some of the goings-on in the dormitories made him think it might be better if his daughter stayed in her room. One of Emily's biographers makes an interesting statement about her relationship to this strait-laced parent. "Her father's death in 1874," he says, "left her without a rudder." We had realized he was stern, but thought he had merely paddled her a time or two.

Outliving her father by twelve years, Emily kept to her room, illegibly scribbling poems on the backs of envelopes

Emily at work

97

and tiny scraps of paper, in a fiendish effort to make things difficult for her editors. She wrote several thousand poems, but only seven were published in her lifetime. It was not that she got them back, with rejection slips. She never mailed them out, which indicated either (1) remarkable modesty, or (2) lack of postage stamps. It is estimated that the total income of her poetic career, for these seven poems, was $6.50. However, her works have sold well since her death. Since she had no children, *somebody* must have made a nice thing out of her books.

In her poems, Emily Dickinson has a way of asking the reader some disconcertingly frank questions. For instance:

> Have you got a brook in your little heart,
> Where bashful flowers blow?[1]

Another, which we blush to quote, especially since it comes from a spinster, is:

> Did the harebell loose her girdle
> To the lover bee?

It is doubtful that Emily ever found out, though she spent many watchful hours in her garden.

She could be remarkably telling (though sometimes it is hard to know what she is telling) in a metaphor. For example:

> He put the belt around my life,—
> I heard the buckle snap.

But she was perhaps at her best in a simple observation of nature, noticing something the rest of us would pass by without seeing. Take the stone:

[1] An electrocardiogram ought to give the answer.

> How happy is the little stone
> That rambles in the road alone.

Have you ever stopped to think, as Emily Dickinson did, how much a little stone enjoys being a little stone? And have you ever seen a little stone rambling in the road alone, perhaps whistling as it jogs along? You haven't? That shows you how much more observant a poet is.

One critic, writing of Emily Dickinson, refers to "the artful cricket in her brain." No wonder she stayed in her room all the time.

XXI

The Rise of Realism

D URING the sixties," says one literary historian, "realism was hovering in the air but refusing to perch." It finally came to rest on William Dean Howells, who was so busy writing he hardly looked up.

William Dean Howells

Howells was a self-made man, as was his most famous character, Silas Lapham. Owing to the poverty of his family, he interrupted his schooling at the age of nine to set type in his father's printing office. The type was pretty heavy for a little boy, and he was always glad to set it somewhere. In his teens he had such a passion for reading that he read himself into a nervous breakdown. It was a pity he had not taken up smoking or drinking or some other habit easier to shake.

He recovered, however, and was fairly healthy until the publication of his first book, a book of poems. This was so poorly received that it caused a relapse.[1] In a fit of despair, he read all of the Waverley novels in a month, scorning anything so easy as committing suicide. Eventually,

---

[1] The book "fell on stony ground." Some of his poems were tender and bruised easily.

however, he found a way to free himself from the reading habit: every time he had the overpowering urge to read a book, he wrote one instead. How often he fought off temptation is indicated by his thirty-six novels, five books of autobiography, nine volumes of criticism, six books of poetry, thirteen books of travel, thirteen volumes of sketches and stories, many plays, and hundreds of articles.

Howells probably edited more magazines than any other American author. These included *The Nation, The Atlantic Monthly, Cosmopolitan,* and *Harper's.* He was also a

Overpowering urge

frequent contributor to these magazines. An astute and impartial critic, he frequently sent himself a printed rejection slip and occasionally one of those encouraging notes: "You have promise. Try us again." This sort of thing, coming from a critic he admired, bucked him up no end.

The realism of Howells emerged in *The Rise of Silas Lapham,* about a paint manufacturer who had been too busy making a fortune to acquire any culture, even a veneer. He embarrasses his marriageable daughters by bragging and shooting his cuffs and using the wrong fork. But in the end, even though it means going bankrupt, he places honor above money. Socialist critics, reading of this honest capitalist, maintain that this is not realism but fantasy.

There is nothing sordid about Howells' realism. Even had he written about the garment industry, he would not have depicted the seamy side. "I write," Howells said, "in such a way as to cause no blush of shame to rise upon the maiden cheek." Penelope and Irene, the daughters of Silas Lapham, are so virtuous, so tolerant of their father, and so thoughtful of each other that parents today are tempted to put the book on the fairy-tale shelf. At any rate, the reader who seeks sex and depravity must look elsewhere.[1]

Howells once said of the people in his realistic novels, "I turned eagerly to some neutral-tinted person who never had any adventure greater than missing the train to Dedham." What he seems not to have realized is that missing the train to Dedham can be a terrifying experience, especially when it is the last train and it means spending the night in Boston. Such a person isn't neutral-tinted, he's as white as a sheet.

Though Howells has been called "a champion of writers of realism," this does not mean that he was the best of them, and wore a diamond-studded belt in token thereof. It means that he wrote articles in their behalf. This may be disappointing to the reader, but, in deference to Howells, let us be realistic.

[1] He need not look far. See Dreiser, Hemingway, O'Neill, and Faulkner, below.

Henry James

The question most often asked, when anyone mentions James, is "James who?" Once this is cleared up, the next thing will probably be a reference to the James brothers, and it is helpful to know, when you are discussing American literature, that these are Henry and William, not Henry and Jesse.

One thing that is confusing about the two brothers is

The James brothers—
Jesse and Henry

that Henry James wrote psychological novels, while William James wrote novel psychology. Another thing that is confusing is the writings of Henry. In *Daisy Miller* and *The American* he was fairly simple and straightforward, but he could hardly wait to start using his "later manner." An example of this follows, from *The Sacred Fount:*

"She's beastly happy?" he broke in getting firmer hold, if not of the real impression he had just been gathering under my eyes, then at least of something he had begun to make out that my argument required. "Well, that *is* the way I see her difference. Her difference, I mean," he added, in his evident wish to work with me, "her difference from her other difference."

Some find James hard to follow. It is not true, however, that a reader once wandered back and forth inside a pair of parentheses, unable to extricate himself, until he died of starvation.[1]

Never much concerned about plot, James developed his technique to such a point that he could write a full-length novel, such as *The Ambassadors,* in which nothing whatever happens—or, if it does, he forgets to tell. He holds the reader spellbound, however, wondering whether the sentence on which he has started will ever come to an end. And there is always the possibility of murder, if one character should manage to talk another to death.

James was known as an "international" novelist, because he usually wrote about Americans in Europe or Europeans in America. In order to get the feel of the thing, he himself was born in New York City but lived most of his life in London. His most amazing feat, during his sojourn in England, was dining out 107 times in a single season. Either he had a large circle of friends or hated the food at home.[2]

In his international novels, characters like Christopher Newman in *The American,* Isabel Archer in *The Portrait of a Lady,* and Daisy Miller in, by coincidence, *Daisy Miller,* are uncultured, unsophisticated Americans who are given a bad time of it by Europeans and ex-Americans who have culture running out of their ears. Daisy Miller is a

---

[1] It was thirst that got him.
[2] Don't be too quick to blame his wife. James was a bachelor.

fine example of the innocent but carefree long-legged American girl who finds Rome full of wolves, descended from Romulus and Remus. She gets sick in the Colosseum but, unlike the many American tourists who have since undergone a similar experience but have had shots for malaria and typhoid, dies. If this sounds simple, one has only to read a few pages of critical analysis to discover how complex it actually is. As a James critic would say, and in fact has said, innocence is a function of intelligence, love unafraid is not usually inarticulate, and James's characters are externalizations of hypothetical subtleties.

Increasingly, James turned from the novel to the short story and novelette. His best-known work in the latter genre is *The Turn of the Screw*, a ghost story which has frightened many a reader who hadn't the slightest notion that (1) the ghosts are not really ghosts but hallucinations of the sexually repressed governess, (2) the beauty of Bly (the old country place) is no more than an ironic value, and (3) it is a moot point whether the pathological or the supernatural predominates.[1]

Henry James died in 1916. Though there have been many attempts, no James revival has been wholly successful.

Ambrose Bierce

Ambrose Bierce made an enviable reputation for saying nasty things about people, especially women, and was

[1] It has become increasingly evident that Edmund Wilson knows far more about *The Turn of the Screw* than Henry James ever did. It is interesting to conjecture the result, if Wilson had written the story and James had interpreted it.

widely read, especially by men. In his best-known book, *The Devil's Dictionary*, he defines marriage as "a community consisting of a master, a mistress, and two slaves, making in all, two." Still in this mathematical vein, one of his characteristic epigrams is: "You are not permitted to kill a woman who has injured you, but nothing forbids you to reflect that she is growing older every minute. You are avenged 1440 times a day." [1]

Some of Bierce's bitterness may have been caused by an unfortunate accident during the Civil War. In the battle for Kennesaw Mountain, he received a musket ball through his head. Though the two holes eventually healed up, Bierce still felt hurt.

As a journalist in San Francisco, Bierce is said to have dipped his pen in acid, and fellow newsmen learned to stand well away so as not to be splattered. He became famous for his cutting remarks, and his definition of FAMOUS in *The Devil's Dictionary* is "conspicuously miserable."

As might be expected, Bierce wrote some grim stories, in which his purpose was to shock the reader. The very title of one of his books, *Cobwebs from an Empty Skull*, does very well as a starter. A good example of one of his gruesome tales is "An Occurrence at Owl Creek Bridge"—as vivid a description of a hanging as you will ever read. It's a tricky story, at first fooling you into thinking the victim gets loose, but everything clears up nicely once you get the hang of it.

Bierce's dates, usually given in parentheses, are (1842–

---

[1] In case you haven't guessed, Bierce was married. His wife referred to him as "my bitter half."

Bierce finding Villa (and vice versa)

1914?), and a question may arise about the question. The fact of the matter is that Bierce, thinking he might get material for some articles, went to Mexico in 1914, looking for the bandit Pancho Villa, and people ever since have been looking for Bierce. Some think he is still alive, though since he would now be more than 120 years old, the number of the faithful is steadily dwindling.[1]

O. Henry

O. Henry is probably the only American writer named after a candy bar. Actually O. Henry was his pen name, thought up while he was in the pen, serving a term for embezzlement.[2] The *O.* stands for nothing, or zero, and

[1] If he found Pancho Villa soon after he arrived in Mexico, he probably died in 1914.

[2] His real name, and the one he should have used on his checks, was William Sydney Porter.

probably reflected O. Henry's estimate of his chances for literary success as he started that three-year stretch behind the bars.[1]

O. Henry's most characteristic work is in *The Four Million,* a collection of short stories about the little people of New York. He sought out the hidden romance in humdrum lives.[2] In "The Gift of the Magi" a young husband sells his beautiful watch to buy his wife some combs to wear in her beautiful hair, and meanwhile the wife sells her hair to pay for a chain to go with her husband's watch. What is so romantic about this? Well, the wife still loves her husband, though he hasn't a watch, and the husband still loves his wife, though she hasn't any hair. And they still have each other, as well as the combs and the watch chain. In "The Furnished Room," a girl from the country, who had failed in her attempt to become a singer, commits suicide in her cheap lodgings. A little later a young man who loves

---

[1] These were not chocolate bars, else O. Henry might have eaten his way out.

[2] Lives of people who hummed and drummed to keep their spirits up.

her and has been trying to find her rents the same room, is maddened by the faint smell of her perfume, and kills himself. Perfume-makers ever since have been trying to duplicate that haunting odor, guaranteed to quicken a man's desire to slash his wrists.[1]

One of O. Henry's specialties is depicting rundown rooming houses. In "The Furnished Room," the housekeeper looks like an "unwholesome surfeited worm," and her voice sounds as if it comes from a throat lined with fur. The rug is threadbare and stained, the upholstery is ragged, and the air is foul and tainted. One of the pleasures of reading an O. Henry story is that when you have finished you look around and decide that home isn't so bad after all.

O. Henry stories are known for their sudden surprise endings. His own ending came quickly, in 1910, at the age of forty-eight, but it was no surprise to those who knew how much he drank.

[1] The young man in the story asphyxiated himself. He couldn't stand the sight of blood.

XXII

The Rise of Naturalism

FOLLOWING closely upon the realists came the naturalists, who thought the realists were not realistic enough. These naturalists, let it be said, are not to be confused with lovers of plants and animals. Probably the most satisfying definition is given in *Webster's New International Dictionary*, which describes a naturalist as "an adherent of naturalism." [1]

American naturalists are supposed to have emulated the French and Russian naturalists, such as E. Zola and I. Turgenev, perhaps hoping to prove that there was just as much drunkenness, crime, lust, and insanity in the United States as in Europe. In general, naturalists thought man was the victim of his environment, depicted squalor at great length,[2] and found the unpleasant fascinating.

Stephen Crane

Stephen Crane was the fourteenth child of a minister.[3] One of the most interesting facts about young Crane is that

[1] An adherent, according to the same helpful source, is "one who adheres."

[2] Also at Winesburg, Ohio.

[3] Not a Mormon, as you might have thought, but a Methodist.

he played on the baseball teams of two colleges, though he never graduated from either institution, probably because he was so busy running from base to base. A sensitive, unorthodox young man, his first love affair was with an older woman to whom he wrote: "You have the most beautiful arms I ever saw. You never should have to wear dresses with sleeves. If I could keep your arms nothing else would count." This confirmed her worst suspicions, and she fled to England, where she married someone for whom she had more general appeal. Crane recovered and married an-

Loved those arms

other, but he frequently dreamt of those well-rounded elbows, gone forever.

His first novel, *Maggie: A Girl of the Streets,* is about a girl who rises from the slums of New York to become a worker in a collar-and-cuff factory and eventually a prostitute. Along the way, she is seduced by a bartender. In the tenement district where she lives, serious questions about life are raised. For instance, to quote a neighbor who hears an uproar in Maggie's room and sticks her head in: "Is yer fader beatin' yer mudder, or yer mudder beatin' yer fader?" With both of these worthies drunk, a third party had to be asked. From this high point the story goes steadily down hill until in the end Maggie winds up at the bottom of the river. Present-day publishers, who would need only an outline of the plot to start dreaming of best-seller lists, will be astonished to learn that Crane could find no one to publish his book and had to bring out this gem of sordidness, sex, and violence at his own expense!

However, he won Instant Success [1] with *The Red Badge of Courage,* possibly because many thought it a sequel to *The Scarlet Letter.* Actually it is the psychological story of a young Civil War soldier who is afraid of being thought a coward, until he gets hit on the head with a rifle butt and wakes up a hero. Crane had no firsthand knowledge of the Civil War, in part because he was born six years after Appomattox. He is supposed to have learned about war from reading Tolstoy, which is no doubt safer but takes longer.

Frank Norris

Frank Norris liked to write of "the raw man, the man with his shirt off, stripped to the buff and fighting for his life." In midwinter, such a man might be fighting just to keep warm. Or, if he had any sense of modesty, he might be trying to get his clothes back.

A fine example of one of Norris's heroes is McTeague,

[1] Just pour in a little water and stir.

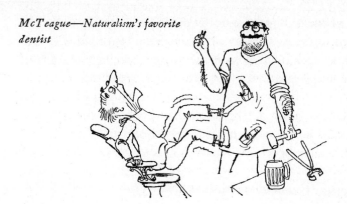

McTeague—Naturalism's favorite dentist

in *McTeague*. A muscular dentist with enormous, hairy hands, he pulls out teeth with his thumb and forefinger, thus saving the overhead of expensive dental equipment. He also effects a considerable economy by never cleaning his bedroom-office, which smells so strongly of beer, bedding, and warmed-over stew, that very little ether is needed to knock out a patient. The reader gets a close-up view not only of a dreary San Francisco street where workers carry "their little pasteboard boxes painted to imitate leather," but of McTeague's dental parlors, right down to "a spot of white caries on the lateral surface of an incisor." Though he spends a good deal of his time drinking beer, playing a concertina, and knocking people down, McTeague is quite successful as a dentist, even without a D.D.S. He finally achieves his lifetime ambition: a huge gold Tooth to hang outside his window. But about this time several things happen which crimp his practice: (1) he loses his license, (2) he kills his wife, and (3) he runs off with his pet canary. It is not true, as one critic has said, that McTeague was "well executed," though he should have been. Actually he died of thirst in the desert. Or so we suppose. The

113

last we see of him he is in the desert, without water, handcuffed to the dead body of a friend he has killed with the same weapon he used on his wife—his bare hands. As McTeague stares stupidly at the horizon, the author seems to be trying to tell us his chances of survival are slim.

Norris's great work was to have been a trilogy about wheat.[1] He wrote two parts, *The Octopus* and *The Pit*, but died before he could write the third part, thus falling a bit short of the whole wheat story.

Little Women, published two years before Frank Norris's birth, was one of the most popular books in America during his youth. Its influence on such a novel as *McTeague* is not readily discernible.

Jack London

Jack London was a two-fisted writer. One can picture him at work—punching a typewriter with rights and lefts until it is flattened. An outdoor man with broad shoulders and a large ego, he liked to stand on a promontory, the wind tossing his luxuriant hair with reckless abandon. And speaking of hair, Jack London had the hairiest chest of any American author until Ernest Hemingway. He usually left his shirt unbuttoned so his admirers would recognize him.

Since London had been a hobo, sailor, oyster pirate, stevedore, drunkard, cannery worker, gold prospector, and rancher, and had got into trouble from the Klondike to the South Seas, he never had to ask himself, "What is there

---

[1] A sociological novel which would have told of the wheat man's burden.

Where men are men and dogs are wolves

to write about?" He was even jailed for vagrancy, and this, along with his feeling that capitalists were underpaying him for his stories, helped make him a Socialist. He continues to be popular in Russia, where he is thought of as typically American in his emphasis on crude force, though more enlightened than, say, the Rockefellers with their emphasis on crude oil.

The heroes of Jack London's books, such as *The Sea Wolf* and *The Call of the Wild*, are all red-blooded— sometimes red-blooded men and sometimes red-blooded dogs. In *The Call of the Wild* the principal character is a dog named Buck, "the dominant primordial beast," that snarls, shows his fangs,[1] and leaps at someone's throat every few pages. Up in Alaska, where Buck pulls a sled when he isn't ripping open a carelessly exposed jugular, men are men and dogs are wolves. When Buck discovers

---

[1] Or Buck teeth.

this latter fact, he joins a wolfpack and lives happily ever after. What a romantic picture he makes, jogging along in the wintry moonlight looking for his evening meal, which is trying to avoid him.

London seems obsessed by wolves. In *White Fang,* he tells of a wolf that goes soft and becomes a household pet. After dealing with a nasty, double-crossing dog known as Lip-lip,[1] White Fang finds human beings not so bad. In *The Sea Wolf* the captain of the *Ghost* is Wolf Larsen, a cross between Captains Ahab and Bligh, whose only human quality is a tendency to headaches. Open the book anywhere and you'll find him beating a seaman to a pulp or refusing to take aboard a couple of former shipmates who are drowning.

After reading Jack London, one feels like eating health foods, signing up for a course in muscle development, or getting a transfusion. The type of blood isn't important, just so it's good and red.

Theodore Dreiser

In novels like *Sister Carrie* and *Jennie Gerhardt,* Theodore Dreiser shocked genteel society by writing sympathetically of women of easy virtue. *Sister Carrie* was published in 1900, when Queen Victoria was still alive, and women of hard virtue were generally preferred.[2]

Then, in *An American Tragedy,* Dreiser showed a young man committing murder and being executed in his effort to gain material success. As a result of the popularity of the

[1] Not only double-crossing but double-lipped.
[2] At least by other women.

book, Dreiser himself gained material success, and it didn't hurt him a bit. Dreiser's homework for the novel included reading a newspaper account of a suspicious-looking drowning, interviewing a condemned murderer at Sing Sing, and consulting a psychiatrist. This last was to learn the psychology of murder and not to get straightened out himself.

What upset many good people about *An American Tragedy* was that it flew in the face of the cherished Amer-

An American tragedy

ican tradition of Horatio Alger. To get ahead, you were supposed to work hard and save your money and stay away from fast women. Dreiser's Clyde Griffiths drowned his pregnant mistress so he could marry a rich society girl and win wealth and position without working for them. Despite the fact that he was convicted of murder and electrocuted, the story set a lot of people thinking. He almost made it, didn't he? Now if he just hadn't written those letters. . . . Maybe Horatio Alger was wrong about toiling onward and upward, and all the rest of it.

Most critics write of Dreiser's prose in superlatives. Ludwig Lewisohn, for example, hails him as "the worst writer of his eminence in the entire history of literature." Dreiser had a year at Indiana University, and presumably took Freshman Composition. Nowhere else could he have learned to construct such a sentence as this: "He delighted to fondle her body evenings; and, leaving the crowded downtown section where traffic clamored and men hurried in a great stress of effort, he would come out through the dusk of the evening to this spot where were vines, in season, and a charming view of the river spreading wide and gray in dark weather, or leaden blue and silver in bright, and feel that he was well stationed and physically happy in life."

This is as good a place as any for the reader to leave Dreiser.

XXIII

New Developments in Poetry

IN our preoccupation with the novel, we have neglected poetry. But then, so has everyone else.

Has poetry been dead since 1882? [1] Are there no new poets, no new poetic farms? [2] As a matter of fact there was such an upsurge of poetry in the second decade of the present century that by 1916 there were more poets than readers of poetry. The surplus was alarming, the Government not as yet having discovered the means of poetry control whereby poets would be paid so much for each poem they agreed not to write.

This unhappy situation was brought about by two revolutionary developments. First, presses sprang up which would print a book of poems if the poet would pay the cost. The cost was rather high because work was slowed down when typesetters became sick to their stomach and had to leave their machines for a few minutes.

The second development was even more ominous. Poets learned that although people would not read their poems, they would pay to hear the poet read them. It was not that people wanted to listen to poets but that they wanted to be seen listening to poets. It was considered Cultural.

[1] No, but Longfellow has.

[2] The word was meant to be *forms*, but it came out *farms* and we rather like it that way.

Vachel Lindsay

One of those who was paid for reading his poems to people was Vachel Lindsay. Sometimes he was not exactly paid but read his poems in exchange for food and lodging. The rate of exchange varied. Before an unenthusiastic audience he might have to read himself hoarse for a cup of coffee.

Lindsay prepared himself by several years of lecturing for the Y.M.C.A. and the Anti-Saloon League. This latter made him accustomed to hostile audiences and developed a certain agility at dodging out back doors. Often he chanted his poems, encouraging his audience to join with him. Peo-

Chant along with Vachel

ple passing by thought a revival meeting was going on inside.[1] Born a generation too soon, he would have prospered on TV with a network program known as Chant Along With Vachel.

A feature of Lindsay's poetry is the emphasis on sound.

[1] A revival of poetry?

In "The Congo," for instance, notice the emphasis on the third word in the explosive line:

Boom, boom, BOOM!

And Lindsay could frighten the wits out of his hearers when he whispered:

Mumbo-Jumbo will hoo-doo you,
Mumbo-Jumbo will hoo-doo you.
Mumbo ... Jumbo ... will ... hoo-doo ... you.

He gave those dots in the last line all he had, and then helpfully ran out into the audience with a bottle of smelling salts.

Lindsay's best poems are about men on the move, such as "General William Booth Enters into Heaven" and "Abraham Lincoln Walks at Midnight." Particularly memorable is his poem on William Jennings Bryan, who rarely walked but ran again and again. To give the reader some idea of Bryan's repetitiousness, Lindsay called the poem "Bryan, Bryan, Bryan, Bryan."

It is in "General William Booth Enters into Heaven" that we find Lindsay at top form in the use of alliteration, as in the opening line, "Booth led boldly with his big bass drum." More nearly complete alliteration might have been achieved had the line read, "Booth bled boldly with his big bass broom." [1] In the same poem, Lindsay indicates which musical instrument one should play while chanting each stanza—bass drum, tambourine, flute, or electric guitar. Chanting a poem while beating a drum would not be too difficult, but chanting lines feelingly and at the same time playing a flute takes talent. Fortunately for the tiring

[1] This makes no sense, but the sound is terrific.

reciter, the final stanza bears the notation: *"Reverently sung, no instruments."*

Vachel Lindsay is easily the noisiest poet in American literature.

Edwin Arlington Robinson

"Robinson's life, like his muse," says one critic, "was overshadowed by gloom." He had the peculiar knack of always seeing the dark side of everything, no matter how hopeful the situation. All about him, he felt, was decay, a feeling that became especially intense when he waited in the dentist's anteroom.

It is fortunate that Tilbury Town, of which Robinson wrote with such brilliant despondency, was a figment of his imagination. Otherwise its suicide rate would have led the nation, and its Chamber of Commerce would have been a Chamber of Horrors. It was full of people like Richard Cory, who for no apparent reason, except perhaps to prove his marksmanship, put a bullet through his head; Miniver Cheevy, who had a bad cough that was likely to be the death of him; and Cliff Klingenhagen, who drank wormwood instead of wine.[1] Anyone in Tilbury Town who laughed was thought to be out of his mind.

One of Robinson's most entertaining poems is "Mr. Flood's Party," about old Eben Flood, who climbs up on a hill above Tilbury Town one night and has a ball, drinking from a jug and carrying on an animated conversation with himself. As the poet says, in a picturesque passage:

[1] Cliff was something of a trial to his friends, who had to keep a bottle of wormwood on hand, just for him.

A quiet evening in Tilbury town

He stood there in the middle of the road,
Like Roland's ghost winding a silent horn.

Luckily for old Eben, there was not much traffic. Had there been, with those silent horns, he would never again have lifted a jug.

The pervasive tone of Robinson's poetry is caught in such a line, in "Credo," as "The black and awful chaos of the night," or, in "Flammonde," "We've each a darkening hill to climb." More than once Robinson wrote, "I cannot find my way." He was always forgetting his flashlight.

Amy Lowell and Edna St. Vincent Millay

Two poets who had much in common were Amy Lowell and Edna St. Vincent Millay. Both were women. But they had their differences, too. For instance, Miss Lowell smoked cigars, while Miss Millay, as she said in one of her poems, burned her candle at both ends.

Amy and Edna

Amy Lowell was an Imagist, and wanted her poems to be "hard and clear." This doesn't make sense, because when a poem is hard it isn't clear and when it's clear it isn't hard. Anyhow, her most famous Imagistic poem is "Patterns," in which she tells of walking down a garden path wearing a fancy brocaded dress. Then she weeps,

> For the lime tree is in blossom
> And one small flower has dropped upon my bosom.[1]

No wonder she wept. There she was, in that nice dress, and a dirty petal came down on her clean bosom. That's the sort of poignant situation that makes for great poetry. The dress, incidentally, went to the cleaner.

Amy Lowell, who never married, was usually delicate in referring to love, but in "Patterns" there is a moment of savage passion when her lover, in uniform, catches up with her on the garden path,

> And the buttons of his waistcoat bruised my body
> as he clasped me.

She had already taken off her stiff brocaded gown, because it was a hot day, but might better have left it on to protect herself from disfiguring bruises. This is one of the hazards of a love affair with a military man. Lest anyone get the wrong idea about Amy Lowell, the whole episode was not only Imagistic but Imaginary.

Edna St. Vincent Millay, too, could be delicate about sex, as when she referred to Euclid, who "looked on Beauty bare." She had the good taste not to go into details about this Greek Peeping Tom.

[1] Amy was a Bostonian, which explains her pronunciation of "bosom" as "bossom." She herself was the stout, bossomy type.

Miss Millay, it has been said, wrote with "rapturous intensity." An example is this intense line in her poem "Recuerdo":

> And you ate an apple, and I ate a pear.

On second thought, this might better be described as an example of her ravenous intensity. She and the man she was with were hungry, after going back and forth all night on a ferry. Not only were they hungry, but they were getting nowhere. So they ate their fruit in silence, except for the smacking noise he made with his apple and the slurping sound she made with her pear. There is a great deal of poignancy about the scene, and the reader is left with deep thoughts about the two lovers.[1]

Nothing Miss Millay ever wrote brought such enthusiastic response as an early poem, "Renascence." The opening lines,

> All I could see from where I stood
> Was three long mountains and a wood,

tug at one's heart with their reference to limited vision and to mountains that are long instead of high. Then there is the pathos of

> The sky, I thought, is not so grand;
> I 'most could touch it with my hand,

with that childlike *'most* and the pathetic underestimating of the distance involved. But what gives the poem its almost hypnotic attraction is the plaintive cry of the poet, dead and in her grave:

> I would I were alive again
> To kiss the fingers of the rain.

[1] Lovers of fruit, that is.

Anyone who would want to get out of a nice quiet grave and kiss the rain, finger by finger, has what it takes to be a major poet.

Miss Millay lived a Bohemian life in Greenwich Village, and what eventually happened to her makes us shudder. As one critic describes it, she "withered on the stalk before gaining fruition." It makes you think twice about going into this poetry-writing game.

Robert Frost

Robert Frost was born in California, and had he not left there as a boy and lived most of his life in New England, it is hard to imagine his writing books with titles like *North*

Robert Frost

of Boston and *New Hampshire*.[1] For a time he tried farming, but a line of poetry would pop into his head just as he started to milk a cow, and he had to go back to the house for pen and paper and often failed to return. This had unfortunate consequences (see "The Death of the Hired Man"). He became recognized as a great poet in America only after he published a book of poems in England. The same thing happened to Shakespeare.

[1] However, he might still have written *Complete Poems*.

In "Mending Wall" Frost says, "Good fences make good neighbors." Anyone who has built a high fence to keep out his neighbor's noisy children will appreciate the wisdom of this observation. On the other hand, in "Birches" he seems to approve of boys shinnying up trees and bending down the branches. This may be all right if the boys stay home and make a shambles of their own trees. But it's a dangerous sort of thing to encourage, according to the S.P.C.B.[1]

The range of Frost's poetry is shown by such representative titles as "The Pasture," "The Tuft of Flowers," "Mowing," "Blueberries," and "The Cow in Apple Time." "I wonder about the trees," he says, in a haunting line that keeps you wondering. His horse often had his doubts, too, as in "Stopping by Woods on a Snowy Evening," when Frost admits:

> My little horse must think it queer
> To stop without a farmhouse near.

But though it was chilly, the horse had a bit of rest before the poet collected his thoughts, wrote three memorable stanzas, and then remembered where he was going.

In his later years, Frost traveled over the country, speaking to college students and collecting honorary degrees from places like Harvard, from which he had failed to graduate.[2] He was an impressive-looking man, one critic remarking that "his works were written in his face." He probably did not mean all his works, but only "Lines."

---

[1] Society for the Prevention of Cruelty to Birches.

[2] After he became famous, he was made a member of the Board of Overseers, to see that this sort of thing didn't happen again.

Carl Sandburg

Before he became a poet, Carl Sandburg drove a milk wagon, served as a porter in a barber shop, shifted scenery in a theater, washed dishes in a hotel, made bricks, and harvested wheat. He was also a door-to-door salesman, movie reviewer, bell ringer, janitor, soldier, and reporter. Which of these occupations best fitted him for poetry has been the subject of a number of scholarly papers, such as "The Influence of Dishwashing on Carl Sandburg's Imagery" and "Brickmaking and the *Weltanschauung* of the Later Sandburg." It is generally agreed that delivering milk provided him with most of the folk materials he published in *The American Songbag*. One of these authentic ballads turned up on the back of a note reading "Leave an extra quart today." [1]

He not only collected folk songs but sang them, accom-

---

[1] Reference to *The American Songbag* reminds us that Sandburg's poetry is often compared to that of Walt Whitman, sometimes known as The American Windbag.

Collected folk songs

panying himself on a guitar.[1] He was the first triple-threat poet, singer, musician on the American scene, and put any number of entertainers who could do only one of these things out of work.

Sandburg saw life clearly, despite an unruly lock of hair that fell down over his eyes. What he saw is indicated by a passage from his famous poem, "Chicago":

> They tell me you are wicked and I believe them, for I
> have seen your painted women under the gas lamps
> luring the farm boys.

This was in 1914, when there were still farm boys and before women learned to use eye shadow correctly and to stand under electric lights.

Sandburg's love for Chicago is further shown by his poetic description of it as "Hog Butcher for the World." This invariably makes a native Chicagoan, now living in California or Florida, homesick for the delicate aroma of the stockyards and the happy cries of animals being led to the slaughter. As Sandburg points out, it is a city that can be proud of its smoke, dust, and gunmen. It's a man's town.

The best known of Sandburg's lines are probably

> The fog comes
> on little cat feet,

which tug at the hearts of cat-lovers. Few know that Sandburg originally wrote "little flat feet." This was during his Socialist phase, when he was thinking less about cats than about the underdog.

Sandburg was a little uncertain about himself, in various

[1] The guitar, in turn, accompanied him everywhere he went.

poems saying "I am the people," "I am the prairie," "I am dust," and "I am a copper wire slung in the air." It is no wonder that one of his poems is entitled "Who Am I?" In this same poem he says, "My name is Truth." Some think he suffered from amnesia.

A somewhat imaginative critic has said, "Under close scrutiny Sandburg's verse reminds us of the blobs of living jelly or plankton brought up by deep-sea dredging." By coincidence, there was a marine biologist who, after looking at the blobs of living jelly and plankton brought up by deep-sea dredging, exclaimed, "This reminds me of Sandburg's verse."

XXIV

Writers of the Twenties

IN the 1920's, most of the writers belonged to the Lost Generation, a group of gay young people who, after a particularly wild party, would wake up in the morning in some strange place, such as Greenwich Village or the Left Bank or Nice, and ask, "Where am I?" They were always trying to find themselves. It seems they had had their moral fiber* loosened by World War I, when it was fashionable for writers to drive ambulances, jolting along at high speeds over rough roads.

F. Scott Fitzgerald

F. Scott Fitzgerald was the spokesman of the Jazz Age, when most people were too busy drinking and dancing to say anything. "You tell 'em, Scott," was about all they could mumble before they slipped to the floor in a drunken stupor.

In such novels as *This Side of Paradise* and *The Great Gatsby,* Fitzgerald depicted the spirit of the hour, which was usually about 4 A.M. His suave young men, impeccably dressed in white flannels and carrying tennis rackets, were always commuting between Princeton and the Plaza in Stutz Bearcats or Locomobiles at devil-may-care speeds.[1] They never sat still for long. It was too uncomfortable, with a large flask in the hip pocket.

As for Fitzgerald's "lacquered maidens," as one critic calls them (probably a misprint for "liquored maidens"), they wore long strings of beads, which helped hide their flat chests, and dresses with waists which were about a foot below where their waists really were and kept everyone guessing. However, their skirts were short, and this was a help. Like Fitzgerald's young men, his young women loved nothing so much as a wild party, which afforded them the opportunity to make lengthy speeches about themselves. Then too, there was always the chance that someone would break the boredom by committing suicide.

There was a good deal of revelry and glitter in the life of Fitzgerald's characters. "I had to sink my yacht to make the guests go home," one impatient host said when it was past his bedtime. A Fitzgerald character usually had plenty more yachts where that one came from, and more guests eager for a midnight swim. Wealth fascinated Fitzgerald, who once commented to Ernest Hemingway that he was interested in the very rich because they are somehow different from other people. "Yes," Hemingway said, "they have more money." This had never occurred to Fitzgerald before, and he went right home and told Zelda.[2]

[1] Of as much as fifty miles per hour. One of his characters at the wheel of a Stutz Bearcat had "a half-sneer on his face," the wind apparently having blown off the other half.

[2] Zelda was his wife, and that was her real name. He also knew a girl named Ginevra.

A good deal of revelry and glitter

There is a striking similarity between Fitzgerald's novels and his own life. Whether this is because he based his novels on his life or because he based his life on his novels is an interesting question, isn't it?

Gertrude Stein

Some of the writers of this period left America and went to live in Paris, thus becoming ex-patriots. One of these was Gertrude Stein, who put words into the mouth of her secretary, Alice B. Toklas.[1] This resulted in *The Autobiography of Alice B. Toklas,* which was really written by Gertrude Stein. If this seems confusing, read some of Gertrude Stein's other books.

Miss Stein could never understand why many people were more interested in her as a person than in her poetry. With her iron-gray hair, cut like a monk's or a Roman senator's, with her dresses made of brown burlap bags, and with her size-twelve shoes, she should have escaped notice. It must have been something she said that made her stand out in a crowd.

Gertrude Stein's style of writing [2] is said to have been influenced by the brushstrokes in a Cézanne painting which hung over her typewriter. She in turn influenced many American writers then in Paris, such as Sherwood Anderson and Ernest Hemingway, who had pictures of Gertrude Stein, hanging, over their typewriters.

[1] Since Gertrude Stein seldom gave her a chance to say anything, many thought her name was Alice B. Talkless.

[2] Actually she had two styles. They were known as her "difficult" style and her "more difficult."

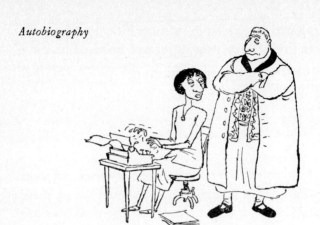

She was said to be an experimentalist, and yet she could sometimes get in a rut, as in her famous line

A rose is a rose is a rose.

Since Miss Stein cunningly left out punctuation and capitals, few readers are aware that she was referring to a friend of hers, named A. Rose, who was unmistakably himself.

Another of her most beautiful and plaintive lines is

Pigeons on the grass alas,

which is frequently printed

Pigeons on the grass, alas.

That gratuitous comma between *grass* and *alas* made Miss Stein furious. By separating the two words, it takes much of the sorrow out of the grass, which was in a sad state because of pigeons. This is made clear in what follows:

Short longer grass short longer longer shorter yellow grass Pigeons large pigeons on the shorter longer yellow grass alas pigeons on the grass.[1]

---

[1] In *Four Saints in Three Acts*, shortly before the exciting scene which opens: "Letting pin in letting let in let in in in in in let in."

What made it so sad, you see, was not just the pigeons on the grass but the large pigeons on the shorter longer yellow grass alas, which had been getting longer longer instead of shorter longer and green greener instead of yellow fellow yellow until the nasty pigeons had taken to nesting on it on it on it on it on it.

Get it?

Ezra Pound

Ezra Pound was not only an ex-patriot in England and France but, later, downright unpatriotic in Italy. He preferred Mussolini to Franklin D. Roosevelt and, since he was not a Republican, was declared insane.

He knew Greek, Latin, French, Italian, Provençal, Japanese, and Chinese, as he frequently hinted in his poems. Thus in a typical passage he says

> We see τὸ καλὸν
> Decreed in the market-place,

Linguist

whereas if he had said

> We see the beautiful
> Decreed in the market-place,

the reader would not have been nearly so impressed with Pound's knowledge of Greek, and the editor would have had no occasion to elaborate in a footnote.

It was Pound who thought up the name Imagists for the Imagists, who had been sitting around helplessly, wondering what to call themselves. But he himself soon left the Imagists and joined a more advanced group, the Vorticists. What attracted him to them was probably the mellifluous and descriptive name of their journal, *Blast*. He wished he had thought of it.

Pound's *Cantos* can be compared with Dante's *Divine Comedy*.[1] The central theme is the decay of civilization, showing how the civilization which produced poets like Homer and Virgil finally got down to Ezra Pound. The *Cantos* influenced T. S. Eliot's *The Waste Land* and depressed countless readers because they thought themselves stupid, not being able to understand.

H. L. Mencken

While other critics collected their prejudices in volumes entitled *Literary Criticism*, H. L. Mencken called his prejudices *Prejudices*. This was probably because he was a specialist in the American language.

Mencken criticized the American masses, or "booboisie," because they didn't subscribe to either *Smart Set* or *The*

[1] In length.

A specialist in the American language

American Mercury, both of which he edited. He also had no use for New England, of which he said: "It began its history as a slaughterhouse of ideas, and it is today not easily distinguishable from a cold-storage plant." [1] New England along about the middle of February—who could argue?

Some think Mencken was opposed to democracy, which he called "the most expensive and nefarious kind of government ever heard of on earth." But it must be remembered that he also wrote: "Government is actually the worst failure of civilized man." So he was really quite objective and impartial, hating all forms of government equally. Almost as interesting to Mencken as government was the relationship of men and women. He defines love as "a wholesale diminishing of disgusts." In case the reader didn't catch it the first time, he goes on to say, "When we are attracted to a person and find his or her

[1] It is not quite true that he had no use for New England. As the above indicates, he thought it could be used for refrigeration.

proximity agreeable, it means that he or she disgusts us less than the average human being disgusts us." Mencken tried hard to be crusty and cynical, but in such a passage his inherent sentimentality and affection for his fellow men shows through.

As for his guiding principle in life, he probably summed it up best in his oft-quoted remark: "I've made it a rule never to drink by daylight and never to refuse a drink after dark." It was this sort of wisdom that caused Mencken to become known as The Sage of Baltimore.

Sinclair Lewis

Sinclair Lewis put Sauk Center, Minnesota, on the map.[1] In *Main Street* he changed the name to Gopher Prairie, probably on the advice of his attorney. His purpose in writing this book, we are told, was "to puncture the egos of smug, self-satisfied Americans." This he did by speaking "blunt truths about the inadequacies of small-town life." How he expected to puncture anything with a blunt truth was never explained.

Before the publication of *Main Street*, Lewis had been the butt of jokes because he was so awkward and homely —"a raw, carrot-topped fellow." [2] The boys gave him such nicknames as Doodle, Mink, Ginger, and Bonfire. Actually his first name was Harry, which he changed to Sinclair so he could be confused with Upton Sinclair. Later he was called Red by his friends, which is a lot better than being called red by your enemies.

[1] About a hundred miles northwest of Minneapolis.
[2] Raw carrots, no doubt.

With the publication of *Main Street,* and even more with the publication of *Babbitt,* Lewis became a Successful Author, which meant that he drank heavily, was twice married and twice divorced, and was rude and insulting in public. Once he made the mistake of being insulting in public to another author, Theodore Dreiser, who considered this plagiarism. Dreiser, never one for half measures, slapped Sinclair Lewis on both cheeks in one of the most famous literary bouts of the century. As Lewis's biographer says: "Nothing had satisfied the public so completely since Rudy Vallee had been struck in the face by a grapefruit." The public has a great sense of fun.

Lewis may not have been much to look at, but he is said to have had "a fine ear." In novels such as *Babbitt,* about George F. Babbitt, a middle-aged real estate broker who praises Prohibition and drinks bootleg whiskey, he has such wonderfully realistic dialogue as

"Shall we have the Gunches for our dinner, next week?"
"Why sure; you bet."

Not much to look at

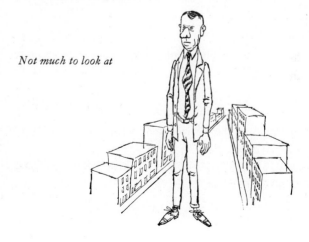

There is a touch of genius about that "you bet," it rings so true to the American vernacular. No wonder Sinclair Lewis won the Nobel Prize.

What *Babbitt* did for the American businessman, *Arrowsmith* did for the American doctor.[1] The main theme of both novels is that money does not pay.

In *Main Street* and *Babbitt,* as well as *Elmer Gantry,* Lewis laid bare the materialism, hypocrisy, and self-seeking of Americans, who loved it. The only writers who have made more money out of showing up Americans for what they are have been British.

---

[1] *Arrowsmith* is full of test tubes and germs, and contains the famous line "The toxin shall not ring tonight."

XXV

Contemporary Drama

IN the twentieth century, American dramatists began to throw off the shackles of convention. Sometimes a dramatist threw a shackle too far and it hit a theatergoer in the third row center.[1]

An interesting development was the Little Theater. If a Little Theater was little enough, it was possible to put on an experimental play and fill it to the rafters [2] with the family and friends of the author. Indeed, one play was described as having played to Standing Room Only because someone at the last moment forgot to bring in the chairs.

The Little Theater was often what came to be known as a theater-in-the-round. This meant that at any given time half the audience was behind the actors. "We're behind you, Jack!" they would cry out enthusiastically. In order to face the audience, actors sometimes kept circling around, like boxers, until they became too dizzy to come out for the third act.

Frequently, in the experimental theater, the stage was bare.[3] The lack of scenery challenged the audience's im-

---

[1] Sometimes, if his aim was good, a critic.

[2] All Little Theaters had to have rafters.

[3] The actors, however, were clothed, unless the theater was very experimental indeed.

agination and cut down expenses. Having no ceiling was another way to reduce overhead. Some of the stage sets were highly impressionistic, perhaps a hand towel tacked onto the wall to suggest a cloud, or a bottle of wine to suggest a bottle of wine.

Eugene O'Neill

The most important dramatist of this period was Eugene O'Neill, the first American dramatist recognized in Europe. When he walked down the Champs Elysées, one Frenchman would say to another, *"Vraiment, c'est Eugène O'Neill, le célèbre écrivain américain!"* [1] Such world-wide recognition led, inevitably, to his being awarded the Nobel Prize.

Before he became a dramatist, O'Neill had a wide variety of experiences, such as being an ordinary seaman on a freighter and spending several months in a tuberculosis sanatorium. Whatever he still needed to know, he learned at Harvard in Professor Baker's "47 Workshop," including why it was called "47 Workshop."

But nothing prepared him for the writing of tragedies so much as his home life. His father was an actor, always on the road and addicted to tippling. His mother was a druggist.[2] His brother was an alcoholic. One of his sons committed suicide and the other took dope. His daughter, who was bound to do something strange with a name like Oona, married Charlie Chaplin, several decades her

[1] In this instance the Frenchman spoken to was named Vraiment, French for Raymond.

[2] No, no; I mean a drug addict.

senior. O'Neill himself, a handsome, brooding man, had "eyes that turned inward," which must have been annoying, and a mustache that drooped at the ends. He left his second wife and two children to run off with an actress, tried to commit suicide, and felt most at home in a saloon called the Hell Hole. After reading a biography of O'Neill, one not only understands his tragedies better but finds them a relief.

O'Neill started by writing one-act plays. Short as they were, he managed to pack in a gratifying amount of horror, loneliness, frustration, disillusionment, and catastrophe. It was his contention that man is doomed and there is no escape—he is doomed if he does and doomed if he doesn't. A few lucky people die young.

One of O'Neill's favorite themes is that of not belonging. This is to be found, for instance, in *The Hairy Ape.* Here Yank, a burly stoker,[1] after being rejected by the Rotarians, Kiwanians, Optimists, and Lions, winds up with the Gorillas, one of whom enthusiastically hugs him to death. Sometimes, however, O'Neill goes to the classical writers for his material, not finding anything morbid enough in the world around him. An example is *Mourning Becomes Electra,* in which O'Neill borrows a family situation involving incest, murder, and suicide from Aeschylus and transfers it from ancient Greece to New England, where it seems right at home.[2]

O'Neill's plays are notable for their unusual devices. In *Strange Interlude,* for example, actors say polite things

---

[1] He did not stoke burly, he stoked engines on a ship.
[2] How Aeschylus got such ideas without reading Freud, as O'Neill did, will always remain a mystery.

to each other but say what they really think in asides which people in the audience hear even if the other actors don't. On the other hand, there are asides among the people in the audience, such as "How much longer is this thing going to last?" which, fortunately, cannot be heard by the actors.[1] In *The Great God Brown* characters wear masks, even though it isn't Halloween. It was at a matinee performance of *The Great God Brown* that the following conversation between two ladies was overheard:

"It's very artistic, isn't it?"
"Yes, but it's good all the same."

But O'Neill's most extraordinary device is used in *The Emperor Jones*, a play about a deposed dictator on a West Indian island who is shot in the end by a silver bullet. While the frightened fellow is fleeing through the jungle, pursued by rebellious natives, tom-toms start thumping at the rate of a normal pulse beat, or about seventy-two a minute, and then go faster and faster. At the end of the play, the audience is exhausted and the drummers usually require a stimulant.

Almost as original as the devices in O'Neill's plays are the titles. For instance there is *Desire Under the Elms*, which causes one to envision a fall scene in New England, with a tired leafraker looking up hopelessly;[2] *The Iceman Cometh*, with its subtle suggestion of a summer day and a housewife with a lisp; and *Lazarus Laughed* ("Ha, ha, ho, ho").

Long Day's Journey into Night, which portrays a family

---

[1] *Strange Interlude* usually runs from about 5 P.M. until 11 P.M., with an intermission for supper, though most persons are too depressed to eat.

[2] That's *exactly* what I envision, it really is.

The Iceman Cometh

of drunks, dope addicts, and misfits constantly quarreling with one another, is obviously autobiographical, even to the point of including an auto. As a matter of fact, most of O'Neill's plays are about himself and his family, except possibly for *Dynamo*, since none of the O'Neills is known to have committed suicide exactly as the hero of the play did, by throwing himself into a dynamo. Such an ingenious method seems not to have occurred to them. Plays like *Anna Christie* and *The Iceman Cometh* are set in saloons, a background O'Neill had been conscientiously researching all his life. In *The Iceman Cometh*, the characters just sit and sit. This is not quite fair; they sit and drink. It is the members of the audience who just sit.[1] At the conclusion of the play there is widespread depression.[2] A statistician has determined that in O'Neill's plays there are twelve murders, eight suicides, twenty-three other deaths, and

[1] This is not quite fair, either.
[2] Even in the theater seats.

seven cases of insanity. No one has had the courage to count the cases of Scotch.

Handsome, rich, and famous, pursued by beautiful women and showered with honors, O'Neill remained gloomy to the end. Life, as he tried to show in his plays, is a dirty trick.

Gloomy to the end

XXVI

Contemporary Fiction

CONTEMPORARY American fiction may be classified as historical, regional, exotic, erotic, erratic, good, and bad, with most works falling into one or another of the last two categories. Sometimes, especially in the short story, the author gives us a slice of life. Perhaps he is carving out a reputation for himself. Then again, he may be sharpening a pencil and the knife slips. "But," as one critic has said, "no matter how thin you slice it, it is still life." [1]

Probably what most characterizes contemporary American fiction is its frankness, though no writer has yet gone so far as to use Frank Ness as his protagonist. The greatest frankness has been in dealing with sex. As this frankness becomes generally accepted, it is increasingly difficult for an author to get his book banned and thereby gain quick recognition and wide readership.

Social consciousness is another feature of contemporary fiction. Most writers are conscious of Injustice and Intolerance and Inhumanity, and therefore are known as the In-Group. Now and then a writer is found who is unconscious, and he is rushed to the hospital for observation. A concern of many writers of fiction is the loss of the individual in

---

[1] This is not to be confused with the still life of painting.

modern society, perhaps from taking a wrong turn on the freeway or forgetting his ZIP Code number. This can be serious, and in most contemporary novels it is.

Ernest Hemingway

Ernest Hemingway began his writing career as a contributor to the Oak Park High School yearbook. About the same time he had the first faint indications of what later qualified him as the leader of the Hairy-Chested School of Writers. Subsequently he continued his journalistic career on a newspaper and then, when he had saved up enough to buy a trench coat, became a foreign correspondent.

Hairy-chested school

Always interested in sports, he is said to have worn boxing gloves while typing, which may account for an occasional blurred image. His most celebrated physical encounter was his bout with Max Eastman, who had intimated that Ernest wore a toupee on his chest. In addition to his prowess as a boxer, he was good at fishing and shooting, and brought back several mounted heads from Africa.

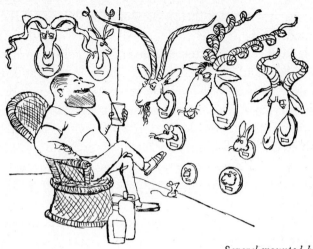

Several mounted heads

During World War I, Hemingway served with an ambulance unit in Italy. He was wounded and decorated with the Croce di Guerra and the Medaglia d'Argento al Valore Militare. Better than medals, because he always carried them with him, were several scars which made interesting conversation pieces. In the hospital, 237 pieces of shrapnel were removed from his legs, Hemingway keeping the tally on a clipboard. Not satisfied with these wounds, he also served as a correspondent in both the Spanish Civil War and World War II, in the latter gaining quite a reputation among our troops for keeping his canteen filled with cognac.

Hemingway had four wives,[1] always being in search of adventure and looking for "the real thing." Or perhaps it was just that he liked women young and vibrant, like the heroines in his books, and so kept trading them in for later models. Besides, unless they were considerably younger

[1] One at a time.

than he, it seemed a little ridiculous for them to call him "Papa."

He believed in shattering conventions and living life up to the hilt, and is therefore a far cry from such as Longfellow, Emerson, and Thoreau. It is hard to imagine Hemingway, who at Key West had fought off sharks to bring in a 468-pound marlin, in a rowboat with Thoreau on Walden Pond, fishing for perch. "Race you to shore, Henry," we can hear him say, standing up in the boat and stripping the shirt from his barrel chest. "Then we'll box ten rounds."

Hemingway's short stories and novels are concerned with the fundamentals of life, such as death. In both *The Sun Also Rises* and *Death in the Afternoon* he writes enthusiastically of bullfighting, there being nothing so beautiful as a dying bull falling to the ground, blood gushing from his wounds.[1] The fleeting instant the matador and the bull stand eyeball-to-eyeball, just before the matador plunges his sword into the bull or the bull plunges his horns into the matador, Hemingway thought of as the Moment of Truth. What the matador thought of we can only guess, perhaps "There must be some easier way to make a living."

Another of his favorite subjects is the satisfying of such elemental urges as hunger and thirst. The characters in *The Sun Also Rises*, a novel set in the bars and bistros of Paris and Spain after World War I, have a hard time satisfying their thirst, but they bravely keep trying. Never

---

[1] When a horse or a matador also was gored, as an aesthetic bonus, he could hardly contain himself. "*Olé!*" he would shout to a Swedish friend who often accompanied him.

have so few drunk so much and still managed to walk in and out of bullrings and bedrooms.

Hemingway also dwells upon love, which he romantically associates with death, one or both of the lovers usually being killed just in the nick of time. This luckily prevents a couple like Frederic Henry and Catherine Barkley, in *A Farewell to Arms,* from living out their lives together in some dull suburb, raising teen-agers and going to PTA meetings. In fact it even prevents them, in this instance, from getting married, which is another device of Hemingway's to make sure that the romance doesn't go out of a love affair.

In *A Farewell to Arms* and *For Whom the Bell Tolls* Hemingway writes brilliantly of battles, for instance the struggle of Robert Jordan and Maria to get into one sleeping bag. This is a striking change from the romantic, unrealistic literature of earlier days, when a man would doff his hat and give up his sleeping bag to a lady.

Hemingway, who was influenced by Sherwood Anderson and Gertrude Stein, in turn influenced countless young writers who will doubtless influence still others, and there is no telling when this will stop. Hemingway's greatest contribution has been in the economy of dialogue, which probably goes back to his early days when he didn't know where the next word was coming from. An example, from *The Sun Also Rises:*

> "It's hot."
> "Hot, my God!"
> "Take off your hat."
> "That's a good idea."

The reader will notice how Hemingway has got rid of the nonessentials and is moving toward that mastery of the writer's art which would permit him also to get rid of the essentials.

We have said nothing of the symbolism of *The Old Man and the Sea.*

William Faulkner

William Faulkner's career as a man of letters began when he served as postmaster of the University of Mississippi. After weeks of struggling to decipher names on envelopes, he blew up. "I can write as well as they can," he said. So he became a writer. His materials were close at hand. "The tools I need for my trade are paper, tobacco, food, and a little whisky," he remarked, slyly putting them in reverse order of importance. Later, when things were going none too well, he discovered he needed still another item: a pencil.

Faulkner's family name was Falkner, and he added the

u just for the heck of it.[1] He may have been influenced by Hawthorne, whose name was originally Hathorne and who added *w* for much the same reason. Faulkner was a short man with a long mustache. He spent most of his life in Oxford, Mississippi, sometimes walking to the corner store, nodding and saying shrewd, earthy things like "Howdy" to the townspeople. Usually, however, he stayed home, sucking on his pipe or on a bottle of bourbon, living the life of a Deep Southern gentleman.

The first of Faulkner's books was a collection of poems called *The Marble Faun*. It was not a success, so he began to write stories and novels peopled with idiots, drunkards, thieves, murderers, prostitutes, and perverts, and won a devoted following among readers who wished to learn how things were going in the South.

Most of Faulkner's novels are set in Yoknapatawpha County, which is really Lafayette County, and in the town of Jefferson, which is really Oxford. The Sartorises, who are really the Sartorises, are an old Southern family on the way down, while the Snopeses are a new Southern family on their way up. Thus they represent the ups and downs of the South. *The Sound and the Fury* introduced another family, the Compsons, who tried to keep up with the Sartorises, never letting them get ahead when it came to lust, incest, and suicide. Somewhat unusual among the Compsons was Benjy, who being a moaning, slobbering idiot was not inclined to sexual immorality, forgery, and violence like the rest of the family. Faulkner was rather partial to idiots. Charles Bon, the idiot in *Absalom, Absalom!*, is

[1] Let us have no facetious comments about the U and the non-U Fa(u)lkners, please.

Faulkner country

about the only person who was not murdered or burned to death when the old plantation house was set fire to. He merely disappeared, and nobody looked very hard for him.

All this time Faulkner was working up to his masterpiece, *Sanctuary*, which has been hailed as "a classic of horror and degradation." Who can forget Popeye,[1] the gangster and pervert? Who can forget the scenes among the moonshiners or in Reba Rivers' bawdy house in Memphis? Who can forget the rape in the corncrib? Some think Faulkner was indebted to Poe for his scenes of grotesque violence, especially those involving Poe white trash.

Quite as important as his masterful picture of the South is Faulkner's prose style, which includes, for instance, the technique of "interior monologue." Anyone sitting near a person thus engaged supposes it to be a growling stomach and pretends not to notice. Then there is Faulkner's almost poetic imagery, as in his story, "A Rose for Emily," when Emily is in a drug store buying some arsenic with which to poison her lover. "The druggist looked down at her," Faulkner writes. "She looked back at him, erect, her face like a strained flag." Anyone who has ever seen a strained flag will understand perfectly.

Closely connected with his prose style is his symbolism. In *The Sound and the Fury* and *Sanctuary*, for instance, every time Faulkner mentions honeysuckle the reader can expect something about sex. In fact the reader can expect something about sex even without any mention of honeysuckle. But this has not lessened Faulkner's popularity.

Faulkner was awarded the Nobel Prize, which forced

---

[1] The way he could shoot people, he should have been called Deadeye.

him reluctantly to give up his seedy tweeds and get into white tie and tails.[1] He had a wide readership abroad. For some reason, his prose is clearer in translation, as anyone knows who has read *As I Lay Dying* in Finnish or *Sanctuary* in Urdu. In an interview, Faulkner was once asked what people were to do who could not understand his writing, even after reading it two or three times. His helpful reply: "Read it four times." Faulkner's prose, it has been said, "requires something of the reader." What this mysterious something is, we have no idea. All we can say is that some readers don't have it.

[1] In his famous Nobel Prize acceptance speech, Faulkner said, "I decline to accept the end of man." Ambiguous as usual, he did not say which end. He liked to leave people wondering.

XXVII

Conclusion

AMERICAN literature did not come to an end with Hemingway and Faulkner, despite rumors to the contrary. Fiction continues with such writers as John Steinbeck, Norman Mailer, Truman Capote, and J. D. Salinger. Its subject matter can perhaps best be summed up by the title of one of Mailer's novels, *The Naked and the Dead*, a book which is not about the members of a nudist colony having a picnic in a cemetery. Drama has taken on new dimensions with the works of Tennessee Williams and Arthur Miller. In *A Streetcar Named Desire* and *Death of a Salesman* these dramatists achieved the impossible by being more depressing than O'Neill. As for poetry, it can safely be said that it has come a long way from Anne Bradstreet and the *Bay Psalm Book* to Allen Ginsberg and his *Howl*.[1]

As we conclude this history of American literature, and look back to its beginnings, we are left with a number of interesting questions. For instance, if he were alive today, what would Cotton Mather think of Jack Kerouac?[2] How much funnier would Ogden Nash seem if he had a name

---

[1] For the source of Ginsberg's howl, see Walt Whitman's "barbaric yawp."

[2] Or, for that matter, what does Jack Kerouac think of Cotton Mather, if he ever does?

like Michael Wigglesworth? And can you imagine the *New England Primer* in paperback with a blonde on the cover?

Another good question, which should always be asked at the end of a survey like this, is: Wither American literature?

ABOUT THE AUTHOR

Richard Armour may be playful and irreverent in his treatment of literature (*Twisted Tales from Shakespeare, The Classics Reclassified,* etc.) and history (*It All Started with Columbus, It All Started with Eve,* etc.), but he bases his satire on an impressive background of scholarship and teaching. A Phi Beta Kappa graduate of Pomona College, and a Ph.D. in English Philology from Harvard University, he has held research fellowships in England and France and has written books of biography and literary criticism. He has taught at a wide variety of institutions, including the University of Texas, Northwestern University, Wells College, the University of Hawaii, and the University of Freiburg, has been Dean of the Faculty at Scripps College, and is now Balch Lecturer in English Literature at Scripps College and Professor of English at the Claremont Graduate School. In addition, he has lectured at scores of colleges and universities in all parts of the country, from the University of Oregon to the University of Rochester.

Describing his double life as a serious scholar and a fiendish satirist, Armour has said that he wears two costumes: cap and gown and cap and bells. His double life is further doubled by his writing both light verse (*Light Armour, Nights with Armour, Our Presidents,* etc.) and prose. He is on the editorial staff of three magazines, is a regular book reviewer for newspapers, and has written books in such various fields as medicine (*The Medical Muse*) and golf (*Golf is a Four-Letter Word*). Though most of his books are bookish, and he has spent much of his life in libraries, he has also drawn on himself and on his family in works such as *Drug Store Days* and *Through Darkest Adolescence*. His books have been translated into French, German, Spanish, Dutch, Italian, Portuguese, Japanese, and Chinese. Scholar-satirist Armour is married, has a son and daughter, and lives in Claremont, California.